MY ANCESTOR
LUNATIC

by Kathy Chater

SOCIETY OF GENEALOGISTS ENTERPRISES LTD.

Published by
Society of Genealogists Enterprises Limited
14 Charterhouse Buildings, Goswell Road
London EC1M 7BA.

© Kathy Chater and the Society of Genealogists 2014.

ISBN: 978-1-907199-32-5

British Library Cataloguing in Publication Data.
A CIP Catalogue record for this book is available from the British Library.

The Society of Genealogists Enterprises Limited is a wholly owned
subsidiary of the Society of Genealogists, a registered charity, no 233701.

About the Author

Kathy Chater has been tracing her own family for forty years. She has a Diploma in Genealogy and the History of the Family from Birkbeck College and a Ph.D. in History from Goldsmith's College. She is the author of *Tracing Your Family Tree in England, Ireland, Scotland and Wales* (Lorenz Books, 2nd ed. 2009), *Tracing Your Huguenot Ancestors* (Pen & Sword, 2012) and *Untold Histories: Black People in England and Wales during the period of the British Slave Trade c. 1660-1807* (Manchester University Press, 2009), which was her doctoral thesis. She also writes articles for magazines and lectures to family history societies.

Cover Image - *Philippe Pinel à la Salpêtrière*, by Tony Robert-Fleury (1837–1911). French doctor Philippe Pinel (1745-1826) releasing lunatics from their chains at the Salpêtrière asylum in Paris in 1795. Public domain image (Wikimedia).

CONTENTS

List of Illustrations

The illustrations on pages 6, 9, 10, 17, 19, 74, 82, 94 and 95 and on 102 (taken by Fiachra Byrne) are in the public domain and have been taken from Wikimedia Commons. The photograph on page 12 is shown with the kind permission of the Bethlem Royal Hospital. Documents shown on pages 30-31 and pages 44-47 are from the Society of Genealogists Library. Other illustrations are from the author's collection.

Acknowledgements

I am grateful to Professor Rab Houston of St Andrews University, Dr James Ross of The National Archives and Susan Snelling of the Library and Museum of Freemasonry. These experts gave me detailed information about Scottish law, forfeiture of suicides' goods in England and Wales and freemasonry respectively. Any errors that remain are my own.

Abbreviations

BRO   Borough Record Office. These are usually called some variation on Local Studies/Heritage Centres/Libraries, etc. They hold the records of a local authority usually dating from the mid-19th century. Some, however, have earlier records because they are towns with an ancient borough charter, like Colchester in Essex.

CRO   County Record Office.

DRO   Diocesan Record Office.

LMA   London Metropolitan Archives.

NRS   National Records of Scotland (formed in 2011 by the merger of the General Register Office for Scotland and the National Archives of Scotland).

RO   Record Office.

TNA   The National Archives.

INTRODUCTION

Mental illness was in the past (and is still to some extent today) regarded as something to be concealed. For this reason, family historians may encounter puzzling silences and absences in their family tree. Genealogists often find a gap in the births of children to a couple. This might be for a number of reasons. The father may have been called to serve in the army or the militia. One of the parents might have been in prison. What is often not considered is that one of the parents might have suffered a period of mental breakdown and been in an institution elsewhere. It must be remembered that many people in the past, as well as in the present, recover and return home. In other cases, a breakdown may have led to permanent incarceration so someone disappears completely.

Many family historians find that one of their ancestors left his or her spouse and set up a family with another person. This is usually assumed to be a kind of informal divorce. But it might be because one of the partners was mentally afflicted and in an asylum. Until 1937, it was not possible to get a divorce on the grounds of insanity unless the bride or groom was insane at the time of the marriage. Isabella Thackeray, wife of the novelist William Makepeace Thackeray, had a breakdown a few years after their marriage and then needed full-time care. Because she was deemed sane at the time of their marriage, he was unable to get a divorce and marry someone else.

It is therefore always worth considering whether an individual ancestor was mentally ill. Over the centuries, there have been many terms for people with mental health problems or whatever is the currently favoured term. I have used lunatic because this was the most frequently used in the past. The word originally had a precise medical definition, and so did other words like 'cretin', 'moron', 'imbecile' or 'idiot' that have now just become general terms of abuse. Currently the word 'disabled' is used to cover a wide range of mental and physical conditions. It blurs the line between mental illness and what is currently termed 'learning difficulties'. Family historians need to distinguish between these two and the range of syndromes which carry some form of intellectual impairment because of the differences in the treatments of the various forms of disability. This will affect where records will be found. I have therefore chosen to use the term *mentally handicapped* for those born with inherent conditions which make them unable to live independently. This was the politically correct term until recently because those who brought it in to replace 'retarded' said that such people were disadvantaged by society's attitudes towards them, which was certainly the case in the past. It was often also believed that people with epilepsy and many deaf people were mentally ill and required special hospitals. These are briefly covered in Chapter 8.

Children's party at the West End Hospital for Diseases of the Nervous System, Paralysis and Epilepsy.

Family historians may also have ancestors in the medical profession who treated or cared for the mentally ill or those with certain disabilities and this book can be used to track them down as well.

What is insanity?

Before proceeding, however, it is worth trying to define mental illness. This is as difficult in the present day as it was in the past. Madness is a continuum - there is no clear-cut defining line. Many people are regarded as odd or eccentric but this does not make them insane. Beliefs about the causes of mental illness and its treatments go through fashions which can determine where the line between sane and mad is drawn. However, three kinds of mental affliction have been recognised for centuries. The first, what is now called *neurosis,* is curable. Past terms include neurasthenia or simply 'nerves'. It includes conditions like OCD (Obsessive Compulsive Disorder); those with chronic anxiety or hypochondria. It appears this last was quite a common affliction among our forebears. Neurotics are in touch with reality, they know something is wrong with them and are capable of changing their behaviour, although this may be difficult.

Psychosis is not curable. Conditions like schizophrenia (literally 'split mind') can be alleviated with medication and other treatments but cannot be cured. What is today labelled a 'personality disorder' might have been attributed to inherent evil, or being possessed by the Devil. Or a person with autism or Asperger's Syndrome might simply be regarded as eccentric. Psychotics are not in touch with the reality that the rest of us recognise and are, except in a very few cases, unable to change their behaviour.

In the past forms of what was called *mental retardation* were also defined as insanity. Down's Syndrome, previously called mongolism, is probably the most obvious example. It is most common in older mothers, and before reliable contraception many women went on having children into their late forties, so a number of such children must have been born. Many would have died young because heart and other physical defects are often linked to this syndrome.

Two other forms of fairly common mental illness should also be mentioned.

It was always regarded as normal for elderly people to become forgetful to a greater or lesser degree. Today we might recognise Alzheimer's Disease in the very severely afflicted but *senile dementia* was a general term for the various illnesses that cause the elderly to lose mental function.

What was called *General Paralysis of the Insane (GPI)* was the result of untreated or incompletely treated venereal disease, which was very common before the 1940s when penicillin became a full cure. Syphilis was treated with mercury until 1909 and then with arsenic. These treatments were unpleasant so when the symptoms abated treatment might be discontinued before the disease was fully cured. If not cured, it

3

could lie dormant for years and then produce balance problems and insanity, usually delusions of grandeur, although these can be produced by other conditions.

Other forms of insanity might also have had a physical cause, like a brain tumour, but it is difficult to make retrospective diagnoses. Even if we do find the case notes of a mentally ill ancestor, doctors in that period would probably have had different beliefs and theories about the causes and symptoms, so something that today would be regarded as significant was ignored and not mentioned. The best example is the illness of King George III. His bouts of insanity are today recognised as caused by a physical disease, porphyria. The most significant symptom is very dark urine, but this was not then regarded as important by the medical men treating the king so it is hardly recorded. This is why genealogists researching mental illness or disability in their families need knowledge about the theories and treatments of their ancestors' time.

What those treating the mentally ill or disabled called themselves has also changed over time. *Alienist* for example, was a term for what today is called a psychiatrist or a psychologist. The term *psychopath* was originally used for someone who studied mental disorders. Today the word describes people with a type of personality disorder that makes them unable to empathise with others. *Sociopath* is becoming the preferred term for this.

CHAPTER ONE

From medieval times to the Restoration (c.1324-1660)

Bartholomew, an English Franciscan friar, wrote a book intended for priests which was published in the late 15th century. He listed the causes of insanity as passion, overwork, thinking too deeply, sorrow, intensive study and fear.

He also noted physical causes from infections, being bitten by a mad dog (rabies), overeating and drinking too much. He distinguished between over-excitement (called mania) and melancholia, which we today would call depression. He recommended a change of environment, both to help people recover their health and to remove them from the cause of their insanity. Music and suitable occupations would also be of benefit. Those who harmed themselves or others should be restrained. All this seems eminently sensible but alongside these thoughtful observations was a belief system that dated back to the ancient Greeks and Romans.

Medieval theories were based on ancient texts rather than observation. The beliefs in these published works about physical and mental health lasted well into the 18th century. Broadly speaking, it was believed that there were four substances in the human body, called 'humours'. These were black bile, yellow bile, phlegm and blood. They were associated with different basic personalities: those with an excess of black bile were melancholy; yellow bile meant an angry, suspicious person; blood gave pride and bravery, sometimes to excess, and phlegmatic people were not a bundle of laughs, but got on with life philosophically. When these humours were more or less equally in balance, the individual was healthy, but when one or another predominated to a great extent or there was a serious lack of a particular humour, sickness, either physical or mental, resulted.

Mental afflictions were largely regarded as part of God's inscrutable plan. There was not much that could be done, although priests were advised to talk to the afflicted to prevent them from falling into the sin of despair or to prevent them from committing crimes.

Hearing voices or seeing visions from heaven, as Joan of Arc said she did, were not regarded, as they would be today, as a possible sign of mental illness, but were investigated to see whether they were of divine or diabolic origin. There is a further possible origin of hallucinations and psychosis. A condition called St Anthony's Fire was caused by ergot poisoning, a fungus which can grow on rye and other cereals if they are not dried and stored properly. This could affect a number of people in a village. As well as producing hallucinations, similar to LSD, there could be physical symptoms, like convulsions, vomiting, diarrhoea and even gangrene affecting fingers and toes.

Joan of Arc.

There was no great distinction between physical and mental illness at this time. The insane were placed in general hospitals, along with the physically ill. Methods of treatment were designed to restore the body's natural balance. Bloodletting, using emetics to make a person vomit, or giving laxatives to 'purge' the body were intended to get rid of excess humours. Gentler methods included using herbs or foods to combat an illness. Someone with a fever that made him hot and sweaty would be given cold dry food. Advice like 'feed a cold and starve a fever' dates back to this period.

At this time, there was also no great distinction between church and state law. Four kinds of insanity were recognised:

1. Those insane from infancy with no periods of sanity, who would probably today be categorised as severely mentally handicapped.
2. Those insane from infancy but with some periods of sanity.
3. Those who had been sane but lost their reason, i.e. those who became mentally ill.
4. Those who were mentally deficient but had some understanding. This seems to mean what today we would understand as having learning difficulties.

Distinctions between the disabled and the ill were made. An idiot was someone who was mentally handicapped, a lunatic someone who became mentally ill. It was believed that the mental state of lunatics was influenced by the waxing and waning of the moon (*luna* in Latin), which was why they had periods of sanity.

There was also not much comprehension of, or differentiation between, those who were of normal intelligence but deaf and had therefore not learned to speak (what was called 'deaf and dumb') and the mentally handicapped who could not understand.

Rich lunatics

The state recognised that it had a role to play in protecting those whose mental shortcomings left them vulnerable to exploitation. The Statute de Prerogativa Regis of 1324 set out the Crown's position as effectively the guardian of the estate and possession of persons unable to administer them themselves because of their mental condition. The responsibility for looking after the assets and welfare of these rich lunatics was devolved to the Lord Chancellor's office and there are many records of these 'Chancery Lunatics' in TNA. In the documents, those that relate to someone with a mental handicap or illness are headed *In re* (Latin for 'in the matter of') *[name] an idiot* or *a lunatic*.

The process was started by a petition from a relative, a lawyer or a creditor of the alleged lunatic asking for an inquisition. From 1833 (see Chapter 3) it might be one of the Chancery's Commissioners who initiated proceedings and medical men usually provided affidavits supporting the petition. The alleged lunatics were then usually examined where they were living, which was often in a private establishment.

The government was also responsible for safeguarding rich minors. This was especially important because of the possibility of marrying a child in order to acquire his or her property and money. Looking after the interest of minors was administered through the Court of Wards and Liveries between 1540-1645. When someone who held land directly from the Crown died, his or her heir had to pay the Crown in order to retain the land. If the heir was under the age of majority (then 21 for boys and 14 for girls) he or she became a ward of the Crown, which retained custody of the land. Among these were some mentally handicapped children. Trustees were appointed to administer the estate.

Pauper lunatics

Care in the community is not just a recent practice. It was mainly the responsibility of the afflicted person's family to care for the sufferer. If they were unable to do so they could pay someone else. The state did not take much interest in the poor. It is difficult to imagine how those whose families did not have the resources to pay for dedicated care, managed. In general mentally ill or handicapped people were looked after by their families. Some might have been taken in by religious houses but others may just have become vagrants, begging for food or money. There must have been a much wider toleration of abnormal behaviour than is accepted today. A clue may be found in the word 'silly', which originally meant 'holy'. The concept of the 'holy fool', one who was deranged but in touch with God and under His special care, may have helped. Hearing voices was not necessarily regarded as a sign of insanity. Undoubtedly, however, many of the mentally handicapped or ill died prematurely, in accidents or by suicide (see Chapter 7). Others may have wound up in prison (see Chapter 6).

Bethlem

The first hospital, and for centuries the only one, dedicated to the poor insane was St Mary of Bethlehem in the City of London, known as Bethlem and corrupted to bedlam to describe a chaotic situation. The Priory of St Mary of Bethlehem was founded in 1247 by Simon FitzMary. It was initially intended to house a religious order whose members would care for sick poor people. Mentally ill patients are first noted in 1377 and by 1403 the majority of the patients were the mentally, rather than the physically, afflicted. The dissolution of the monasteries in 1533 during the

Reformation meant that the priory no longer existed and the Mayor and the Corporation of the City of London bought the site from Henry VIII in 1547. By now the hospital seems to have cared only for the mentally ill. Although the Aldermen attempted to run the hospital, they found it too difficult and in 1574 it was transferred to the same management as the nearby Bridewell. Bridewell was called a hospital, but it was in effect a prison where 'lewd women' and the like were punished.

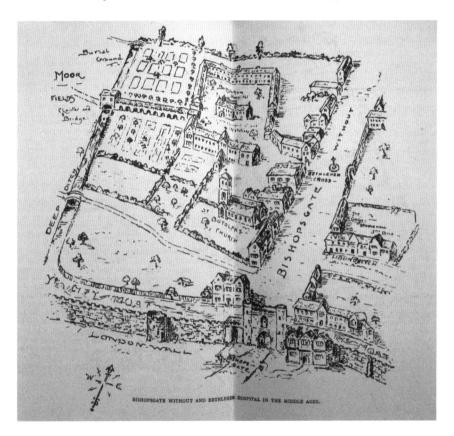

Original Bethlem Hospital. Bishopsgate.

For some 400 years Bethlem was the only public hospital to care for the insane in England, although care may not be the right word. Only the most severely afflicted and dangerous were likely to be there and they were generally just restrained, either physically or by the use of drugs. Furthermore, until the 1720s, Bethlem was not supposed to admit incurables. Patients were discharged, either cured or because they were 'incurable lunatics'. It is clear that some of the better-off Bethlem patients were then put into the private establishments run by the doctors who worked there, like Dr Helkiah Crooke (1613-34), but what happened to the poorer people is not known.

Recovered patients from Bethlem who could not return to their families' care had a special badge to show they had been patients, which was designed to elicit sympathy and help. Men were called Tom o'Bedlam and women Bess o'Bedlam. However, conmen might steal or acquire these badges and use them. These imposters were called Abram Men, after a ward in Bethlem. It was customary for these ex-Bethlem patients and the fraudsters to wear distinctive clothing, decorated with ribbons, feathers and scraps of fabric. They may occasionally be mentioned in court cases.

Tom o'Bedlam.

The Tudors and Stuarts

The dissolution of the monasteries meant that functions of the Roman Catholic Church, such as caring for the sick, were transferred to individual parishes. It became the responsibility of the Vestry to arrange care for the sick among their parishioners, so at this point references to paying for the care of the mentally, as well as the physically, ill may appear in parish accounts. Unfortunately, very few parish records have survived from this early period.

It is also from this time that occasional references to private madhouses are found. Individuals began to care for the mentally ill and handicapped as a business, charging for looking after someone that a family found too difficult to cope with. Some seem to have been clergymen, taking one or two people into their homes. It was thought that the power of prayer would restore people to their senses.

Apart from this, there was not much change in how the insane were classified and treated. The view that mental illness was part of God's plan continued after the Reformation - with a significant difference. The Devil became a much more important figure and the growth of extreme Protestantism meant that the insane were often regarded as those who had given in to the machinations of the Devil. To a greater extent than before people were believed to have brought madness on themselves. This had particular influence on the treatment of suicides and what happened to their property after their deaths (see Chapter 7). With the waning of Puritanism in the late 17th century, there was a growth of interest in possible physical causes of madness, which led on to the next stage in the treatment of the insane.

Treatments

In this period the main ways of treating lunacy were the same as those used to treat physical illness: bleeding, emetics to make the person vomit or purgatives. They might also be kept on a 'low diet', which did not contain meat, thought to inflame the passions. All these had the aim of re-balancing the body's humours or expelling bad influences but they also weakened patients who became more docile and easier to manage. Restraints like chains or straitjackets were used to prevent the violent from hurting themselves or others. Beating might also be used in the hope of driving out bad spirits.

There were also gentler folk remedies using plants, dating back to Anglo-Saxon times. Tying clove wort around a lunatic's neck with a red thread when the moon is on the wane was supposed to cure madness. A number of herbals were written in the 16th century and these suggest a range of plants and herbs which could be used to treat mental illness. In his *Herbal* of 1597 John Gerard recommended the smell of basil. He noted that this 'taketh away sorrowfulness, which cometh of melancholy'. He also said that the flowers and leaves of borage put into wine would 'drive away all sadness, dulnesse and melancholy'.

Finding records

During this period, it is unlikely that there will be records relating to anyone who was mentally ill or handicapped unless they were rich or they were involved in a newsworthy event. There were no newspapers of the kind we are familiar with, but broadsheets and pamphlets relating amazing events or individuals' experiences were published. These are scattered in a number of repositories, but the British Library is a good starting point to see if an event involving an ancestor was covered.

Bethlem Hospital records start in 1557. The early ones are mainly to do with the administration of the establishment. There are admission registers from 1638 but they do not describe individual cases until 1816. The records are in the archives at the hospital, which is now located in Beckenham, Kent. There is also a museum and art gallery with objects and artworks on the same site.

Most other records for this period are in TNA. There are online research guides under the general heading Mental Health, covering *Asylum Inmates*, *Disability* and *Mental Health*.

Chancery Lunatics are primarily found in TNA in C 211, which contains commissions and inquisitions to determine lunacy (1627-1932). The papers in this class are in bundles arranged alphabetically by the individual's surname and the names are in the online catalogue. The documents are in Latin until 1649, then in English during the Commonwealth period and back to Latin from 1660-1733. There are also few from Ireland. C 33 consists of books recording the decrees of the Court of Chancery, including the final judgements in cases between 1544-1875. C 38 contains reports to the court from 1544-1875 concerning a number of matters, such as disputes about the administration of the estates of deceased persons, lunatics and wards of court. C 103 contains a miscellaneous collection of private papers given to Chancery between 1250-1859 as evidence in various cases. This covers a huge range of subjects. C141 has a number of cases.

Inquisitions post mortem are not to be confused with coroners' inquests. They took place after the death of a property owner in order to determine whether the Crown was entitled to anything. They are held in various series in TNA. They are all now indexed and many have been published. C 142 has miscellaneous inquisitions from c. 1485-c.1649, including a number relating to people described as 'lunatic' or 'idiot'. Copies of these are held in E 150 and include *inquisitions post mortem* held by an escheator between c1485-c1603.

The records of the Court of Wards and Liveries (1540-1645) are in WARD. If, after an *inquisition post mortem* had been held, the heir was found to be a minor, copies of the papers would be passed to the Court of Wards and Liveries. These duplicates are held in WARD 7, which contains cases relating to people described as 'lunatic' or 'idiot'. WARD 9 contains miscellaneous documents, mainly related to the administration of wardships which may have further information. See the TNA research guide *Land Inheritance in the Court of Wards and Liveries 1540-1645*, which is under the general heading Courts of Law.

Some parts of the country had separate jurisdictions. The Duchy of Lancaster (DL 7) and the palatinates of Durham (DURH 3), Lancaster (PL 5) and Chester (CHES 3) held their own *inquisitions post mortem*. The Palatinate of Chester included lands in Cheshire and Flint.

Disputes about the conclusions of an inquisition were called 'traverses'. The early Chancery ones are in C 43 and C 44. CHES 7 hold traverses from the Palatinate of Chester.

Wills and probate. A long period, more than a few months, between the death of an individual and the proving of the will may indicate that it was disputed. There are many grounds on which a will might be contested, but one of the more common is a claim that the testator was not mentally fit at the time of making or signing his or her will.

Until 1858 wills were proved in church courts. The lowest level were archdeaconry courts and the next level commissary or consistory courts. Above them were the Prerogative Courts of York (PCY) and Armagh (PCA) and the highest was the Prerogative Court of Canterbury (PCC). Disputes about wills might be pursued in the church courts and/or civil courts, most commonly Chancery but other possibilities include the Court of King's Bench and the Court of Common Pleas. The entry Books of Caveats (PROB 40) in TNA will indicate if a caveat was entered and litigation initiated between 1666-1858. Death duty registers (1796-1811 and 1796-1903) include references to law suits. These may not have been on the grounds of mental incapacity so further research will be necessary. PCC wills and documents relating to their administration are in TNA. Appeals relating to these wills were heard in the Court of Arches, whose records are in Lambeth Palace Library. PCY wills and related documents are in the Borthwick Institute of Historical Research and wills of the lower courts and related documents are usually in the CRO, but there are still a few places that maintain a separate DRO, e.g. Lichfield. PCA original wills and papers were held in the Four Courts office in Dublin and were destroyed by a fire there in 1922. However, copies from local registries and other documentation have survived. The whole area of probate is a very complicated subject. TNA has a number of research guides which mainly relate to PCC wills but give advice about those proved in lower courts.

Until 1838 English law gave nuncupative wills, those which were simply death-bed statements before witnesses of how a person wanted to dispose of his or her belongings, equal status with those which were properly signed and witnessed. What the dying individual said had to be written up as soon as possible. This, of course, often led to claims that illness had made the person incapable of understanding what he or she was saying, made them susceptible to undue mental pressure or was simply a fraudulent concoction to benefit those at the deathbed.

Further Reading

H. E. Bell, *An Introduction to the History and Records of the Courts of Wards and Liveries* (Cambridge University Press, 1953, pbk, 2012). This covers all aspects of the Court's work.
Dorian Gerhold, *Courts of equity: a guide to Chancery and other legal records for local and family historians* (Pinhorn Handbooks, 1994).
Karen Grannum & Nigel Taylor *Wills & Probate Records; a guide for family historians* (A&C Black, 2009).
J. A. Guy, *The Court of Star Chamber and its Records to the Reign of Elizabeth I* (HMSO, 1985).

CHAPTER TWO
The long 18th century (1660-1815)

T he Restoration of Charles II in 1660 not only brought an end to Puritan influence, it signalled the beginnings of a significant interest in science, making observations and experiments to deduce the real causes of phenomena rather than regarding ancient texts as having all the answers. This was gradually extended into medicine. The belief that mental illness had a physical cause began to be paramount. The influence of the Puritans waned, but religious writers continued to regard insanity as the result of excess passions or sin and the medieval ideas of humours still strongly influenced treatments.

There was an increasing recognition that insanity could be cured, not just contained or managed. At the beginning of this period, doctors treated both physical and mental illnesses but as time went on specialists in the mind began to emerge. They were called 'mad doctors' and the private establishments they ran were called 'madhouses'. Most records from private asylums have not survived, or indeed may never have been kept in the first place, but there are a few surviving records of these early institutions.

Westover's madhouse in Wedmore, Somerset, was established in 1689 by John Westover, whose father had been a physician, in the grounds of his own house, where he boarded mentally afflicted patients. He also made visits to outside patients up to about 10 miles away. Westover kept a journal from 1686-1701, which shows that he treated both physically and mentally ill patients. It has been transcribed and put on line, with an appendix listing all his in-patients.

In Fishponds, a suburb of Bristol, Joseph Mason Jnr was the son of a doctor who treated both physical and mental illness. Although the younger Joseph

Mason does not seem to have had any formal qualifications, he took over his father's practice in 1738 and specialised in the mentally ill. His establishment was initially known as Mason's Madhouse, but later became Fishponds House. Mason's granddaughter married Dr George Bompas and the Asylum passed to members of the Cox and Bompas families. The Asylum closed in 1850, when the patients were transferred to the Borough Lunatic Asylum nearby.

Parish authorities also used private establishments for those who were beyond their limited resources. The belief that the insane had to be removed from the situation that caused their insanity gained ground from the middle of the 18th century. This led to an increase in private madhouses and then the establishment of public asylums.

In 1774 a major piece of legislation came into effect, introducing a system of regulation and inspection. This Act for Regulating Private Madhouses required private establishments in the metropolitan area to be inspected and licensed by five Commissioners who all had to be Fellows of the Royal College of Physicians. In the provinces, local Justices of the Peace had these responsibilities. The Act further required that anyone who looked after more than one lunatic be licensed and that the keepers of private establishments receive a certificate from a medical practitioner that any person being admitted was a lunatic. This was in response to many examples of abuses, like men having their wives put into an asylum because they wished to live with another woman. Families might have an awkward person confined for a variety of reasons, even for being converted to a different religion. The penalty for having more than one insane person on the premises without a licence was £500. Anyone who took a person into an establishment without certification from a doctor could be fined £100. Paupers, however, were excluded from the Act, so this did not apply to workhouses and parish infirmaries, nor did it apply to Bethlem and other charitable hospitals.

The madness of King George III

It was the apparent mental breakdown of George III in 1788 that triggered a major growth of interest in theories about the causes and treatment of mental illness and also caused the government to start to take a keener interest in mental health.

The idea that the king of Britain, the head of the empire on which the sun never set, could have been struck down by God with insanity was unthinkable. It is now suggested that he suffered from porphyria, a genetic condition which produces both physical and mental symptoms. The way the king was treated reveals the range of theories about causes and cures that were then on offer. Initially he was treated by his own physicians, who tried the standard methods of the time: bleeding, purging with strong laxatives and blistering - applying heated cups to the body to raise blisters and 'draw out the humours'. They also dosed him with arsenic and antimony. When these failed, a number of specialists were invited to suggest ways of curing the monarch. People also wrote in with their theories and suggestions for cures.

Rowlandson Cupping.

The mad-doctor who was credited with curing the king was Francis Willis, a clergyman who kept a private madhouse in Lincolnshire. His treatment was also very traditional. He was of the old, religious school that thought excessive passion created insanity and his way of curing relied on subduing patients to his will. In this, he was strongly influenced by the theories of Franz Mesmer (1734-1815), who taught that there were natural energy forces that could be harnessed and moved through channels in the body to effect cures. Mesmer's treatment involved using the gaze and movements of the hands near the body or the laying on of hands to direct the practitioner's will and intention in order to achieve results. Willis fixed his patients with his eye and punished them for displaying symptoms of insanity by periods in the straitjacket. George III was also isolated from his family, who were not allowed to visit him, because of the belief that removing patients from the environment which had caused their madness was beneficial. The king apparently recovered from this bout of insanity that afflicted him in 1788 but it was followed by another breakdown in his health in 1801 and by 1811 he had become permanently mad.

Private madhouses

It was not just the well-to-do who used private madhouses. For those who could not pay for care, or if the burden of looking after the lunatic was too great, the only alternative was the parish authorities, who might place a person in a private establishment. William Holland, rector of Over Stowey in Somerset, noted in his diary on 5 December 1799 'The madman in the Poorhouse is outrageous... The man is chained and lies on straw.' Later there were discussions about paying to send him to an asylum in Bristol, but there were suspicions that he had fits when it suited him so this did not happen. This example nicely encapsulates the alternatives. As long as the insane person was not dangerous to himself or others, the workhouse or the infirmary attached to it was where an individual remained under restraint if necessary. If the parish authorities could not cope, they could pay for the person to be cared for in Bethlem or a private madhouse but, because this would involve spending the ratepayers' money, it was undertaken as a last resort when the individual became a danger to himself or others.

Parish records or surviving family account books of the better-off may contain regular payments to either a named individual or an establishment. If these are not family members, it is worth investigating to see if the person was licensed to care for lunatics or the place mentioned is a private asylum. Most of the private establishments were called 'House', like Laverstock House, near Salisbury in Wiltshire, or a similar name, like Haydock Lodge in Lancaster. This meant that families who placed relatives there could say that the individual was 'at So-and-So House' for his health, leaving it unsaid whether this was physical or mental illness.

Many private madhouses were family businesses, run for two or three generations. Laverstock House, for example, was run by the Finch family who had other houses in Wiltshire and London. Initially many were set up by medical doctors, but their descendants might simply have inherited the family business and not offered much in the way of treatment. Completely unqualified people could set up an establishment. The details of the career of Thomas Warburton, who kept two madhouses in Bethnal Green, are given differently by contemporary sources. One, an ex-patient, says he was a runaway butcher's boy who fled to London after fathering a bastard and then was employed in a private madhouse, where he made extra income by supplying the inmates with alcohol, and married the owner's widow to get the business. This was no bar to being called in to examine George III - who sensibly took one look at him and demanded that he be sent away. In 1827 a Parliamentary select committee exposed the unprofessional and neglectful way he ran his madhouses. He claimed to have a medical superintendent, but could not remember his name. Warburton, however, made enough money for his son to be educated as a doctor and the establishments run by the Warburtons continued until 1920.

Many of the smaller private madhouses did not provide much treatment. They might only be licensed to take a few patients and simply provided a short-term change of scene. The young and heartbroken, for example, might be placed there after a love affair finished unhappily. Alternatively someone whose state made them too demanding to be looked after in a busy home or an elderly and embarrassingly demented relative might get more dedicated care here. The novelist Jane Austen's uncle and a brother were cared for privately because her mother was too busy running the vicarage and the family smallholding to be able to cope with afflicted family members as well.

The beginnings of public asylums

Until the beginning of the 18th century, Bethlem remained the only public asylum in the country. It was rebuilt in Moorfields in the 1680s and people could visit it to see the lunatics, leaving money to help support them. It was not until 1770 that regarding the mentally ill here as an entertaining spectacle ended.

Bethlem at Moorfields.

The second public asylum was the Bethel Hospital, built in Norwich in 1713 from a charitable bequest. Then in 1725 Thomas Guy stipulated that the hospital in London endowed under his will was to have provision specifically for incurable lunatics. Between 1750-1800, asylums were either built or planned in several major towns and cities. Physical treatment was usually free in public hospitals but this was not always extended to the mentally ill. Costs were met from a variety of sources. The standard way of funding a public hospital was by subscription. People would contribute a certain amount a year and would be allowed to nominate a number of patients, according to the size of their payment. Medical staff would also be allocated a certain number of places. Most asylums also took private patients, who subsidised the poor. Other funding might come from charity donations. Family historians who find legacies left to asylums might suspect that this may have been in gratitude for care given either to the donor or to a member of his or her family. Parish authorities were also charged if they wanted to use the hospital for parishioners.

These first public asylums were generally small and built inside towns and cities. St Luke's Hospital in London was opened in Finsbury in 1751. Manchester Lunatic Hospital and Asylum was adjacent to the infirmary. It was opened in 1766 with the asylum for private patients and the lunatic hospital for paupers so the two sections of society were kept carefully aware of their social standing.

As is usually the case with public provision, it was done as cheaply as possible. Those in charge often had little knowledge of treatments and might exploit their position to, for example, sell food intended for the patients and substitute inferior victuals, pocketing the profit. The attendants were poorly paid and unskilled. Medical staff might visit rarely, as they had their own private practices and many also had a private madhouse which received the bulk of their attention. Dr William Battie of St Luke's in London had two thriving private asylums in nearby Islington and Dr Charles Best of the York Asylum had a private practice in nearby Acomb.

However, it is always examples of mismanagement and fraud that receive the most publicity. The majority of institutions were probably run frugally by people doing their best with limited resources. Dr Battie was conscientious and well-respected but Dr Best was shamed by the investigations into his management of the York Asylum. Under the 1774 Act magistrates were given the right to inspect private asylums, which had to be registered at the Quarter Sessions. They were recommended to make unannounced inspections. They were not required to visit public establishments. Indeed, magistrates had no right of entry. The magistrate Geoffrey Higgins was alerted to the conditions there after he committed a pauper to the institution but in order for Higgins and his colleagues to gain access to the York Asylum, whose bad practices they exposed in 1792, they had to become subscribers. The investigation heard allegations of serious mistreatment, including rape and murder, of the inmates; of financial embezzlement and fraud; of cruel and filthy conditions for the inmates and faking records to conceal deaths. A convenient fire destroyed the records while the inquiry was going on. This major scandal led to reform.

The abuses found there led to the government conducting a series of inquiries between 1815-19 into the treatment of the insane. This paved the way for the next major phase, the growth of public asylums, which is examined in the next chapter.

Treatment

Willis was not alone in believing that excessive passion created insanity. There was a school of thought that said religious 'enthusiasm' provoked madness. After all, George Fox (1624-1691), founder of the Religious Society of Friends, heard an 'inner voice' telling him what to do and he suffered, by his own admission, from mental torment and depression. He told a magistrate that he ought to 'tremble' at the name of the Lord, hence his denomination's nickname of 'Quakers'. Many of the millenarianist sects who believed the end of the world was nigh and who went in for speaking in tongues, prophesying and visions were regarded as insane by those who did not share their beliefs. Even John Wesley's early followers were tarred with the same brush. The dramatic accounts of the tortures of hell that awaited sinners, according to Methodist preachers, was dangerous to the sanity of their hearers, who fainted or became convinced they were damned. Wesley himself was interested in insanity and recorded treatments that he and others tried. Most of these were folk remedies, like infusing ivy leaves in vinegar and rubbing the sufferer's head with the liquid.

One of the responses to the loss of self-control by the religiously inspired was a growing belief throughout the 18th century that insanity was linked to how the mind responded to experiences. Conclusions could be either correct or incorrect. The insane were not physically ill, nor possessed by the Devil, just deluded and mistaken in their interpretations. The aim of what was called moral treatment or moral management was to re-programme the mind and re-educate the individual's thinking processes. Patients were treated with kindness and persuasion rather than violence and restraints. In the York Retreat, the Quaker asylum that was set up after the death of a Quaker in the notorious York Asylum, this regime was used. A system of rewards and punishments, like that used to socialise children into behaving acceptably, was employed. Restraints were only used when the patient was in danger of damaging himself or others and never for the convenience of the staff. It had a high success rate, although it must be noted that the Retreat was quite selective about the patients it admitted.

The late eighteenth century was the beginning of the division between what were called 'heroic' treatments, which involved physical methods which could be quite violent, and the gentler, less dramatic interventions of talking, reasoning with the insane and working with them towards a cure or at least alleviation of their problems. Among the pioneers of these 'moral' treatments was William Tuke, who set up The Retreat. He was actually a merchant, not a medical practitioner. About the same time Dr Philippe Pinel at the Bicêtre and Salpêtrière hospitals in Paris was also setting free those who had been chained up and bringing in a kinder regime. William's son Samuel Tuke's account of The Retreat (published in 1813) and Pinel's works became influential in Britain.

No one method - heroic or moral - displaced the other and in the following centuries: which was used on an ancestor would depend on what the doctors in a particular establishment favoured. Generally speaking, the poorer you were the less likely you were to have the most recent treatments or the most expensive. This could save patients from some very bizarre heroic methods - mentioned in the next chapter - but might mean people were simply left to their own devices, especially if they were not troublesome. When you find an ancestor in a particular establishment, it is worth checking out what school of thought the medical staff there followed.

Finding records

Workhouses were usually the first point at which poor lunatics were assessed. Some might be picked up as vagrants and will therefore appear in settlement examinations. Alternatively, one of the parish authorities or a member of the individual's family would bring the person in, and a settlement examination might be conducted in case the individual - and the expense of care - could be removed to another parish. Vestry members were reluctant to spend ratepayers' money unnecessarily, so would usually wait a while to see whether this was a passing episode or likely to be chronic. A doctor would be called in say whether the sufferer should go into an asylum and a Justice of the Peace or a local clergyman (until 1889) would confirm that incarceration was necessary. Information will therefore be found initially in the workhouse minutes and then in the accounts of the overseer of the poor. These records are usually in CROs and BROs.

Chancery Lunatics. The government continued to monitor the treatment of rich lunatics and these records will be in TNA in the C 211 series. There is an index to names (IND 1/17612) covering 1648-1853. Some petitions are included in C17/55 from people seeking to have a lunacy commission held on an individual between 1719 to 1733 but these are not listed or indexed so it is a question of going through them individually. In J 117 there are miscellaneous bonds and papers relating to all kinds of business, including some matters related to lunatics between 1707-1967. See also the Finding Records section in Chapter 1.

Wills and probate See Chapter 1.

Asylums MH 51/734 in TNA contains a list of institutions caring for the insane between c. 1201-1966.

Private madhouses. Before 1774, there is not much official information about private madhouses. In the very early days, they would only be mentioned when something catastrophic happened. Nothing would have been known about the service the Reverend John Ashbourne offered in Norton, Suffolk. His establishment is known only because in 1661 he was killed by one of his ex-patients. Chapbooks, broadsheets, pamphlets and, later in this period, newspapers will provide this kind of information. From 1774, licences for people running care services should be recorded in Quarter Sessions records held in CROs and BROs.

Between 1798 and 1812 the government kept a County Register of these establishments, with a list of their patients. This is in TNA MH 51/735, arranged by county. CROs may also have records of private madhouses and this will probably appear on A2A. Try both the name of the madhouse and the proprietor. There are a few in the Wellcome Library for the History of Medicine, which has the Ticehurst archive (soon to be digitised), and there are some in other repositories, like the Westover journal and related papers in Somerset Heritage Centre. The Studymore website can help by providing the names of the owners and the name of the madhouse, usually with the location of records.

John Westover's journal is on: **www.tutton.org/content/Westover_journal.pdf**

An 18th century Gloucestershire Diary: the Journal of Dr. Joseph Mason, proprietor of the Fishponds Private Lunatics Asylum April-December 1763 has been transcribed and edited by Dawn R. Phillips and H. Temple Phillips. The original MSS is in the University of Bristol Medical Library nd there is a photocopy of a typescript in Bristol Record Office, 'B' Bond Warehouse, Smeaton Road, Bristol BS1 6NX. **www.bristol.gov.uk/recordoffice**

Further Reading

Henry Horwitz, *Chancery Equity Records and Proceedings 1600-1800* (PRO, 1998) Richard Hunter & Ida MacAlpine *George III and the Mad Business* was published in 1969 but is currently out of print. Hunter & MacAlpine were the first to suggest that George III suffered from porphyria. The book has an account of George III's illness and treatment with additional sections on 18th century madhouses.

Allan Ingram (ed.) *Patterns of Madness in the Eighteenth Century: a Reader* (Liverpool University Press, 1998) is an anthology of writings by sufferers from mental illness, describing their experiences of insanity and treatments for it, and of mad-doctors describing cases and how they treated them.

Roy Porter *Madmen: a social history of madhouses, mad-doctors and lunatics* (Tempus, 2004) was originally published in 1987 as *Mind-Forg'd Manacles: a History of Madness in England from the Restoration to the Regency*.

CHAPTER THREE
The 19th century to World War I

A great deal of mental health care provision continued to be privately run but the 19th century was the age of the public asylum. Although some places had established charitable asylums in the 18th century, the government began to recognise the need for some kind of public provision. An Act of 1808 encouraged the setting up of county asylums but it was not until 1845 that this was made mandatory. In 1844 a report by the Metropolitan Commissioners in Lunacy, chaired by Anthony Ashley Cooper, Earl of Shaftesbury, found to their astonished horror that there was only one small asylum at Haverfordwest and one private licensed house for the whole of Wales. There was no public provision at all for the 1,177 pauper lunatics in Wales.

The first public asylums, generally with a small number of patients, had usually been set up in the middle of a town or city, often next to or near hospitals treating physical illnesses. In the early part of the 19th century there were so few public asylums that parish officials generally had to continue to send the poor insane they could not cope with to private madhouses. As the number of public asylums grew, the poor were increasingly lodged there, although some parishes continued to use private provision.

Essex County Asylum.

Following the 1845 Act, larger establishments, usually in the open countryside, were constructed. This was partly because more space was needed for the large number of patients who began to be admitted, but also because it was believed that the mentally ill needed to be segregated and the countryside was better for them. These institutions became small, self-sufficient communities. Asylums aimed to give their inmates work both to keep them occupied and to lessen the costs of running the establishment. Most, for example, produced a large proportion of their food with the more tractable patients doing the work of raising pigs, looking after and milking cows and growing vegetables. Women patients did some of this, but were also employed in doing the laundry and cleaning the building. Men might also be engaged in maintenance work around the asylum. This isolation meant that the mentally ill were kept out of sight and became institutionalised, knowing nothing else.

Following the scandals exposed at the York Asylum and a campaign by Quaker reformers, Bethlem Hospital was the subject of an enquiry in 1815. The commissioners found abuses, exemplified by James Norris, an American marine with a violent streak, who had been confined and chained in a sort of cage for ten years to the point that his muscles had atrophied. The medical staff, who were supposed to offer treatment, were incompetent. Dr Thomas Munro, whose father and grandfather before him had been the medical superintendent, simply continued their century-old practices, like bleeding, purging and emetics. He was the proprietor of a number of private madhouses and rarely visited Bethlem. When he did, he examined only a few patients. The enquiry, and

Bethlem at Southwark.

continuing public criticism, produced a threat of legislation, which prompted the governors to set up an internal investigation into the administration and finally to sack Dr Munro and the apothecary, John Haslam. In 1816 the hospital moved from its crumbling and dilapidated premises in Moorfields to St George's Fields. Visitors, especially from overseas, praised its design, its airy exercises facilities and the fact that each inmate had a separate cell. This new site included a separate criminal wing (see Chapter 6).

Although it is not entirely clear why, the number of people diagnosed as insane increased over the 19th century. Some people argue that there was a true increase in mental illness because of industrialisation and other causes. Other people argue that it was the growth of madhouses and asylums that caused more people to be deemed in need of them. All the people employed in this expanding empire needed to be kept busy so behaviour that had previously been regarded as eccentric was now classified as pathological. There is, perhaps, a parallel with counselling. Today a lot of people are trained to be counsellors and as the number of counsellors increases so do the conditions for which people are told they need to be counselled.

Legislation

All these new establishments had to be regulated and the 19th century saw a raft of new laws introduced, many of which created new records and thus sources of information for researchers. In 1815 and 1819 two minor Acts made it compulsory for private madhouses to submit the details of patients' dates of entry and discharge to the county authorities, along with medical certificates confirming the patients' insanity. In 1828 two pieces of legislation, the County Asylum Act and the Madhouse Act were passed. Under the first Act, JPs had to send an annual return of admissions, discharges and deaths in the asylums they visited to the Home Secretary. The Home Secretary could appoint anyone he chose to visit any facility treating mental patients.

Under the second Act, the Home Secretary was also to appoint fifteen Metropolitan Commissioners in Lunacy to make quarterly inspections of private madhouses and mental hospitals in the London area. They were to produce an annual report. Bethlem Hospital was an exception to this law.

In 1832 the task of appointing Metropolitan Commissioners passed to the Lord Chancellor and instead of just medically qualified people, the Commissioners were also to include those who were legally qualified.

In 1833 the government passed an Act which authorised the Lord Chancellor to appoint trustees to administer the estate of a Chancery Lunatic. Two medical men and a barrister were also appointed to visit all the Chancery Lunatics and report on their condition.

In 1834 the Poor Law Amendment Act included a provision that dangerous lunatics could be detained in workhouses for a maximum of only 14 days. This meant that parish authorities could no longer simply use restraint, chaining up a deranged and unmanageable person to save the expense of transferring him or her to a madhouse or asylum. The Boards of Guardians of Poor Law Unions after 1834 often had contracts with an individual private establishment for their lunatics, which might be a long way from the home parish.

From 1842 Chancery Lunatics became the responsibility of two barristers, called the Commissioners in Lunacy. A major report on every asylum in the country was commissioned. This was to be carried out by the Metropolitan Commissioners and their findings were published in 1844. From 1845, although there continued to be more interest in the rich than in the poor, the remit of the Metropolitan Commissioners of Asylums was extended to investigate the conditions of the poor insane all over the country. The title of Chancery's Commissioners in Lunacy was changed to Masters in Lunacy. The Commissioners started to publish annual reports of their findings. These did not name individuals but they occasionally mention incidents that might have resulted in criminal proceedings, e.g. people looking after more mentally ill or disabled patients than they were licensed for, or incidents of abuse. As well as inspections by the Commissioners and by magistrates who were recommended to make unannounced inspections, asylums also had Committees of Visitors, local lay people, who might also issue reports.

Although single lunatics, those who were cared for alone, often by relatives, were not included in any legislation, the Commissioners became increasingly involved in monitoring their welfare. A private register of single lunatics was set up in 1845 by Lord Shaftesbury, the chairman of the lunacy commissioners from 1834-1885, but the entries in this were voluntary and depended on the commissioners being notified. Very few people did. Shaftesbury hoped that each single lunatic could be visited annually by a commissioner, but this proved too big a task to undertake systematically.

In 1853 among the provisions of the Act for the Regulation of Proceedings under Commissions of Lunacy was the abolition of the necessity for a jury to hear a case, if this was agreed. This made the process both faster and cheaper.

In July 1861 the government published a survey listing all the inmates of workhouses who had been there for more than five years. Most, of course, were old or physically unable to work, but among them are a number simply described as 'insane', 'idiot', 'imbecile' or 'weak intellect'. The publication, arranged by county and then individual workhouse, gives names, the length of time each person had been an inmate and why they were there. There is also a column for those who had been brought up in a District or Workhouse school.

The Lunacy Act of 1890 introduced 'reception orders'. People could be put into asylums for their own and others' safety. The orders had to be made by a specialised Justice of the Peace and lasted one year. Detention could be continued after a year, if necessary, by submitting reports to the Lunacy Commission. This Act also created the Court of Protection, which was given jurisdiction over people who were unable to administer their own affairs.

Business records

There are other non-governmental sources of information about the management of the financial affairs of someone declared lunatic.

In 1717 the Bank of England took over the management of government funded debt (gilt-edged stocks). Abstracts of wills were made of those who died with monies in the public funds, as well as abstracts of the orders made for stockholders who became bankrupt or who were declared lunatic. In 1822, for example, Thomas Metcalfe of Ripon was possessed of a considerable amount of government stock, worth about

There are the Sums of

£ 10153 . 1 . 10   three p Cent Reduced Ann^s

1000   three p Cent Cons^d D^o

✗ 2625   New Four p Cent Ann^s

Standing in the Name of Thomas Metcalfe of Ripon Yorkshire Esquire who is become a Lunatic as appears in an Order of the Court of Chancery dated the 19th Novem^r 1822 and by which It is Ordered that the Accountant General Secretary & Deputy Secretary of the Bank do transfer the said Annuities into the Name of the Accountant General of the Court of Chancery In Trust in this Matter & do receive the Dividends (if any) due & pay the same into the Bank on the Credit of this Matter

Order with the Accountant

R_g 3938   3 Decem^r 1822   J White

No 5605 Reverend Miles Moor of Rayleigh no Sf^t Essex   Died Possessed of

f° 31064 £ 2100 New fours   101 4   £ 2126 5

Sworn under And by his Will dated 23^d November 1820. Attested
£ 5000 by two Witnesses Appointed Henry Ellison Sole Executor to whom probate was granted 29th November 1822 therein described of Sutton in the County of Essex Clerk   Identified as per aff^t No 435

In the Will are the following Words
First I direct all my just debts funeral expences and the expences of and incident to the probate of this my will to be paid
Item I give to my Wife Mary the sum of Eleven hundred pounds five per cent navy annuities now

Bank of England wills.

Nº 90505.

There is the Sum of £25. 4 ⅌ Cent Annuities
standing in the Name of William Mitchell of Southampton
Row Russell Square Gentleman Who is become a Lunatic
as appears by Letters Patent under the Great Seal of
Great Britain dated 4th June 1824 therein named and
described William Mitchell residing at Hope Street
Hammersmith in Middlesex, And by which the
Custody of the Person of the said Lunatic and also
the management of his Estate and Effects is granted
to Ann Mitchell Widow, who as Committee may
receive the Dividends due and to grow due on the
said Annuities

Aff⁰ of Identity Cf. 344.

By an Order of Lord Eldon the Hand
dated 17 Aug⁵ 1824. In the Matter of
William Mitchell a Lunatic. His
Lordship with order that the Accomp=
tant Treasury or Deputy Treasury
of the Bank do transfer the Sum of
£25. 4 ⅌ Cent Consols & and Annuities
into the Name of the Petitioner Ann
Mitchell, & that the said Accomp=
tant Treasury, Deputy Treasury or
one of the Cashiers of the Bank, do
receive the Dividends due & to accrue
due thereon & pay the same to the said
Petitioner, Subject to further Order
— Order with M⁺ Secretary Bent.
Eldon 3 ⅌ 1824.

The above £25. 4 ⅌ being transferred
& gone to Warrant, is now to be received
in Money, together with all Dividends
due thereon as appears by further Order
with the Accomptant. Eldon 19 May 1825.

Reg⁺ 1690

Eldon. 19 Aug⁺ 1824.

Nº 90618 John Francis Legge of Urchfont
no Aff⁺ Wiltshire Surgeon Dec⁴ possessed of

fo. 22078 £1600 Reduced 947 £1584 —

Sworn Under
£2000.

Eleanor Legge, Widow
the Sole Executrix in this
died 28 June 1825 as ⅌
Probate. fol. 3815 from which
Henry Joseph Legge
of Hollis Fields Eny Surry Widower
the surviving Executor
3 July 1865 ⅌

And by his Will dated 17th July 1824 Unattested
Appointed his Wife Eleanor Legge now the
Widow and Relict Sole Executrix to whom
probate was granted at Doctors Commons
17th August 1824 (therein also described of Edward
Street Blackfriars Road in the County of Surry and
a Surgeon in his Majestys Navy)

In the Will are the following words
I bequeath to my wife Eleanor Legge the Interest
of all property now belonging or which may
hereafter belong to me during her natural life
and should she die before her mother Eleanor

£14,000. Having been declared lunatic by the Court of Chancery on 19 November 1822, it was ordered that the Accountant General, Secretary or Deputy Secretary of the Bank should transfer the annuities and dividends to the Bank on trust.

Alternatively, someone might have the official authority to act on behalf of another person. In 1824 the Bank noted the sum of £25 of 4% Annuities and related dividends in the name of William Mitchell, a Gentlemen of Southampton Row, Russell Square (having been declared Lunatic by Letters of the Great Seal of Britain) were to be transferred to Ann Mitchell, widow, who 'had custody of the person of the said lunatic and the management of his estate and effects'. He was described as residing at Hope Street, Hammersmith, which suggests that he was not living at home but being cared for in a private establishment. Ann Mitchell was most likely related to him, but she may have been someone who made a living out of caring for a 'single lunatic'.

Companies which issued shares, like the railways companies, might also have to make arrangements if one of their shareholders was found mentally unfit to manage their own affairs. For example, the Great Western Railway (founded in 1835), like any other company with shareholders, started a series of registers listing the transfer of stock and the change of shareholders. The GWR registers for 1869 and 1872 show a note of the orders relating to shares held by Thomas Kirby of Witham, Kingston-upon-Hull, who was 'of unsound mind' as stated in an 'Office Copy Report and Fiat [a formal authorisation] as to the fortune and maintenance of a Lunatic and his family'. Power of Attorney to manage the estate was granted to the Accountant General William Russell.

It was not just testators or shareholders who might be mentally unfit. In 1864 Charles Kennedy 'a Lunatic' was replaced as executor or administrator in dealing with the estate of John Reid Jackson. The GWR registers note that in 1914 persons instructed by an Order of Lunacy for the application of the estate of Peter Cator renounced, on his behalf, his duties as executor of the will of Francis Alfred Lyall, a shareholder of the GWR. Consequently Letters of Administration were granted to the attorney acting on behalf of the sole beneficiary to the original will until Peter Cator should become of sound mind or the beneficiary himself was in a position to apply for administration.

Wills

After 1858 the administration of probate was transferred from the church courts to the government. Wills were proved in the Court of Probate for England and Wales. It is not easy to find records relating to disputes heard in this Court. A solicitor's bill among family papers gave the first indication of trouble in the Hall family.

In 1922 Amy Louise Hall died in Camberwell House lunatic asylum leaving her whole estate to a cousin, Alice Maude Wrightson. Robert Charles Hall, Arthur Hall, Mary Ethel Hall, Alice Esther Hall and Mrs Margaret Mary Thomas entered a caveat against the provisions of the wills, which they lost. Miss Wrightson then sued them all for money she claimed they were withholding from her. The case was brought in the High Court of Justice Probate, Divorce and Admiralty Division (Probate). A protracted legal case, which the Halls lost, followed and they were left with a large bill from their solicitors. Details of the case have not survived in the records of the Probate court, but the case was well covered in local newspapers where Amy Hall had lived.

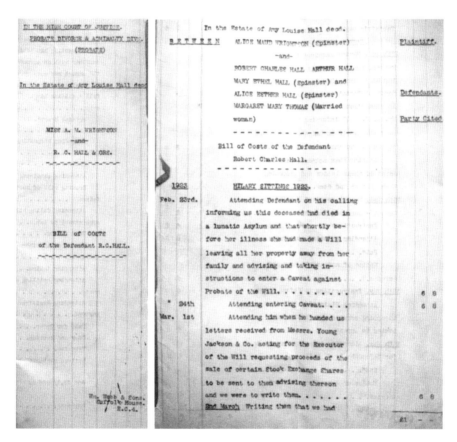

Solicitor's bill - Hall accounts.

Life in an asylum

As the number of public asylums grew, the charges actually decreased. Littlemore Asylum in Oxfordshire's annual fees were £22 19s 10d (1829), £16 13s 8d (1842), £15 18s 6d (1843) and £16 13s 8d (1844, 1845, 1846). Typical fees for a public asylum in the mid-19th century were £11 14s 6d per annum for 1st class patients; £6 5s 6d for 2nd class and £2 1s 10d for the 3rd class. Those who came from another county were charged £3 0s 0d.

Day-to-day life can be imagined from the annual reports that many public asylums published. The Suffolk Lunatic Asylum opened in 1829. From 1837 the governors published an annual report. By 1843 there were about 200 patients. The governors published how much was spent annually.

TABLE SHEWING THE WEEKLY AND ANNUAL CHARGE FOR EACH PATIENT, SINCE THE ASYLUM OPENED.

YEARS.	1st. Quarter.		2nd. Quarter.		3rd. Quarter.		4th. Quarter.		Annual Charges.		
	s.	d.	s.	d.	s.	d.	s.	d.	£.	s.	d.
1829	12	2	8	2	7	0	8	2	22	19	10
1830	7	7	6	5	5	5	7	0	17	1	3
1831	7	0	7	7	5	10	7	0	17	16	5
1832	6	5	5	10	5	10	5	10	15	10	11
1833	5	10	5	10	5	3	5	10	14	15	9
1834	5	10	5	3	5	10	5	10	14	15	9
1835	7	0	5	3	4	8	5	10	14	15	9
1836	5	10	5	3	5	10	5	10	14	15	9
1837	7	0	5	10	5	10	5	10	15	18	6
1838	6	5	5	10	5	10	6	5	15	18	6
1839	7	0	6	5	5	10	6	5	16	13	8
1840	7	0	6	5	6	5	7	0	17	8	10
1841	7	0	6	5	6	5	7	0	17	8	10
1842	7	0	6	5	5	10	6	5	16	13	8
1843	6	5	5	10	5	10	6	5	15	18	6

SUFFOLK LUNATIC ASYLUM.

[J. LODER, Printer, Woodbridge.]

FINIS.

25

Annual expenses.

They also detailed the weekly menu which was probably similar in other county asylums. Breakfast was always the same: milk gruel (made with about an ounce of oatmeal) and 6oz of bread per patient. For dinner (eaten in the middle of the day) on Monday and Thursday men had 6oz of meat, women had 5oz, and vegetables, plus 4oz bread and ¾ pint beer. On Tuesdays and Fridays there was vegetable soup made from the previous day's leftovers, with additional meat and 6oz bread each. On Wednesdays and Saturday men got 1lb of suet dumpling and women ¾ lb, plus ¾ pint beer. Sunday dinner was bread and cheese, men had 8oz bread and women 7oz, with 1½ oz cheese and ¾ pint beer.

HEADS OF EXPENDITURE,

For the Year ending 31st. December, 1843.

		£.	s	d.
Meat, lbs, ...	33,798	644	5	11
Bread, loaves 4½lbs. each	22,597	509	7	3
Flour, stones	1,030	93	14	6
Milk, gallons	2,916	75	15	1
Butter, lbs.	2,780	118	16	11
Eggs		22	7	
Oatmeal, lbs.	4,377	36	1	
Tea, lbs.	403	89	7	5
Cheese, lbs.	5,743	135	5	5
Soap, lbs.	4,768	89	13	9
Grocery		182	4	6
Candles, lbs.	1,077	25	12	11
Coals, tons.	219	201	16	
Wood, loads	17	17		
Medicines, Wine, and Spirits		38	4	7
Beer		224	19	6
Clothing		447		
Sundries		48	11	10
Salaries and Wages		693	8	6
Total. . . .	£.	3,693	12	1

THERE HAVE BEEN REMOVED WITHIN THE YEAR—

	£.	s.	d.
2 1st. Class Patients, at a loss of	23	9	0
1 2nd. Class	6	5	6
3 3rd. Class	6	5	6
4 Out-County Patients	12	0	0
£.	48	0	0

Leaving, now, only 4 Out County Patients in the House and 7 Boarders.—The remainder are all County Paupers.

Expenses - 1843 accounts.

The evening meal, called supper, was ½ lb bread for men, 7oz for women plus 1½ oz cheese and ¾ pint beer on Monday, Wednesday, Thursday and Saturday. On Sunday, Tuesday and Friday ¾ oz butter, and ½ pint tea were substituted for the cheese and beer.

Although this diet was probably supplemented by fruit grown in the grounds, it still looks horribly stodgy and boring to us, but it was more or less what poor people outside the asylums were eating and in some cases may well have been better than their families could afford. Plus, as Suffolk noted, 'We find the continued comfort of the Arnott's stoves, they work very well and we are enabled by them to keep the house pretty generally throughout at a temperature between 55 and 60 degrees.'

In their leisure time patients might have musical instruments to play and games like bagatelle, backgammon, playing cards and draughts to amuse them. In 1862 the report of the Committee of Visitors to Littlemore Asylum included a note by the minister that he had brought in his Magic Lantern to entertain the inmates. He added that this was a novelty only to the new patients but he was continuing with his reading classes.

Of course there were abuses. Very poor quality, cheap meat might be provided to cut costs, or provisions might be sold or stolen by the staff, leaving the patients to go without but this was not typical. Campaigners emphasise abuses in a system when they want to change it but most people, then as now, seem to have been doing the best they could with limited resources.

Patients' records

From 1845 records of patients began to be much better kept. Standard printed admission registers were produced giving headings for date of admission, name of patient, sex, class (private or pauper), age, marital status, occupation, who paid, name and relationship of the person who referred the patient to the asylum. They might also include details of the patient's history of physical and mental health, the cause of insanity and whether the patient was epileptic or an idiot. The discharged category might include four outcomes with the relevant dates: *recovered*; *relieved*, i.e. improved but not cured and often with an address to which the person was discharged; *not improved*, usually with the address of another institution to which the person was transferred (occasionally *escaped*) and finally *died*. In addition, there might be medical journals and casebooks detailing treatment and charting the patient's progress or lack of it. A register recording occasions when mechanical restraint was used to subdue an unmanageable patient might be kept. Registers of official visits or doctors' visits would be kept separately from those of the patients' family members and friends. And, as with all institutions, account books, detailing income and expenditure, will provide a great deal of information. Naturally the records of private asylums, like Ticehurst or the East India Company's establishments (see Chapter 5), tend to keep the best and most extensive records because they had more demanding customers, but public asylums had similar records.

Societies and Charities

An organisation called the Alleged Lunatics' Friends Society (ALFS) was formed in 1845 by Richard Paternoster, whose father had put him into a private madhouse after a disagreement about money, and other people, who also felt that they or their relatives had been abused by the system. ALFS campaigned for changes in the laws on lunacy which allowed people to be locked away without proper evidence and helped to bring test cases to court. It also worked to improve conditions in asylums and to offer help to discharged patients. Although this society was wound up in the 1860s, it paved the way for a number of charities working in the field of mental health.

In 1873 the Lunacy Law Reform Association (LLRA) began to campaign against wrongful confinement and for public rather than private provision of mental health care. The founder, Louisa Lowe, had been put into a madhouse by her husband, a vicar, because of her belief in spiritualism, plus (she thought) he wanted to get his hands on her money. It closed in 1885.

The first mental health charity to help people in the community was set up in 1879 by the Rev. Henry Hawkins, the chaplain at an asylum in Middlesex. It was originally entitled The After-care Association for Poor and Friendless Female Convalescents on Leaving Asylums for the Insane. It set up residential homes and soon moved into preventative care, providing accommodation for people thought to be in danger of mental illness. It later became the Mental After Care Association (MACA) and today it is called Together. Since then, there have been numerous other charities established to help people with mental conditions. Family historians may find letters or other documents from a charity among old papers.

Causes of mental illness

Along with the proliferation of asylums and madhouses went a variety of theories about the causes of mental illness and its treatment. These divided into the physical and the psychological schools. It must be emphasised that all of these methods apparently worked for some people. The problem then (and to a certain extent now) is that practitioners become fixated on one method of treatment that has worked with particular individuals and then apply it to everyone.

Moral insanity

Previously mental illness had been seen largely as the result of physical causes but as both interest in mental health as a specialist branch of medicine and religious revivals grew, there was an increasing emphasis on the morals of the insane. James Pritchard (1786-1848) first used the term 'moral insanity' in 1835. He believed that in the same way as intellectual faculties could become diseased, moral faculties could also be affected. He thought this was especially applicable to criminals. However, in Ticehurst and other asylums where the well-to-do were accommodated, 'moral insanity' became the most common diagnosis. It is not always certain how this was being defined, but it could cover all kinds of behaviour thought unbecoming or likely to bring shame on a family, such as a teenage girl in danger of developing an unsuitable relationship. This concept was enshrined in law by the 1913 Mental Deficiency Act, which defined 'moral defectives' as those who from an early age had displayed 'some kind of mental defect, coupled with a strong vicious or criminal propensities on which punishment has little or no effect'. This catch-all term could be used for any behaviour considered socially unacceptable.

Masturbation, for example, was also called onanism, after the sin of Onan in the Bible who 'spilled his seed upon the ground', i,e. practised the withdrawal method of contraception. Also called self-abuse, in the 18th century this was thought to cause physical weakness and lassitude in young men and women or even blindness. It was not until the 19th century that medical opinion included mental weakness, or insanity, in the list of the baneful effects of masturbation. Because of the Biblical condemnation, this was seen as a moral failing. In 1858 six of the male patients admitted to Colney Hatch Asylum in North London were there because of 'masturbation'.

Treatments

Phrenology was a late 18th century idea which was taken up in the early 19th century. In 1796 the German doctor Franz Joseph Gall claimed that the sizes of areas of the skull reflected the strength or weakness of different aspects of the mind. He identified 27, associated with such qualities as benevolence, religious feeling, pride and even murder. Having one's bumps read became a fashionable pastime between 1810-1840, and there were medical practitioners who believed that this could help to diagnosis mental illness. You may find notes on patients saying that, for example, their organ or faculty of benevolence is well- or under-developed Alongside this, there were many people who believed that facial features reflected the underlying mental qualities of an individual. There is some truth in this. Most syndromes that produce cranial or facial distortions, like Down's, also involve some mental retardation. If an ancestor's appearance is described or there is a photograph and seems abnormal, it might be worth checking whether this is due to a genetic condition which was not recognised at the time.

In the 18th century, it became fashionable to visit spas to drink water whose minerals gave it special health-giving properties. From the 19th century this was extended to using water as a way of curing mental illness. Sufferers did not just drink the liquid. They might be given a 'bath of surprise', by being led to a concealed reservoir of water with a cover which gave way when the patient stepped on to it. Douche baths, shower baths and the use of jets of water directed on to part of the body might also be used. At the extreme end, water could be poured upon them in huge amounts and they might be left for up to an hour under the torrent. The idea was to rearrange the disordered nerves and brain cells. Another early 19th century invention was the swing, which rocked a patient back and forth. This therapy was extended into another way of giving the brain a good jolt, called the whirligig, which spun a strapped-in patient around.

Sedatives, principally laudanum (a derivative of opium), or calomel (made from mercury) could be used to calm patients but it was difficult to give them drugs unless they co-operated. The hypodermic syringe, which allowed drugs to be delivered to unconscious or uncooperative patients was not developed until 1853.

Galvanism is the use of a mild electric current to contract a muscle. The process was discovered by Luigi Galvani (1737-1798). It was used for many medical purposes, including occasionally to treat mental illness and epilepsy. In 1865 a doctor advised that 'the safest mode of employing electricity is to place the patient on the insulating stool, and subject him to the electric bath, and to draw sparks from different parts when thus insulated, and placed in connection with the prime conductor.' it is not clear whether water in the 'bath' was also involved, but don't try this at home.

Moral cures

Less physically radical methods, like the moral treatment pioneered in the 18th century, continued to be used and gained ground, especially in public asylums. Dr John Conolly, who became the resident physician at the Hanwell Asylum in West London in 1839, refused to allow restraints like manacles, chains or straitjackets to be routinely used.

Henry Maudsley (1835-1918) was superintendent of the Manchester Royal Lunatic Asylum and another important person in the history of treatment. Although originally militantly in favour of the physical causes of insanity, he came to believe that madness was the result of both innate factors (nature) and environmental factors (nurture). The money he left to found what became the Maudsley Hospital in London was used to carry on these ideas, which are still extremely influential.

Mesmerism, very fashionable in the 18th century, had become rather discredited by the 19th. In 1843 James Braid, a Scottish physician proposed the term hypnosis for a technique derived from mesmerism. Hypnotism is short for 'neuro-hypnotism' or sleep of the nerves and it gained a substantial following.

Finding records

County asylum records may be in a number of places. Consult the Hospital Records Database to discover the current name of an institution and the whereabouts of its records. In TNA, MH 51/735 contains the county register of asylums outside London between 1798-1812. This includes the names of inmates. Most asylums, like Colney Hatch asylum in Friern Barnet in Middlesex, had their own burial grounds and the registers should be with the hospital's records. The bodies of some of the inmates, however, might be claimed by relatives to be buried in churchyards or cemeteries elsewhere.

Hospital records are increasingly being digitised and put on the internet. The admission records of Prestwich Asylum from 1951-1901, for example, are on Find My Past and the patient records of the Worcester County Lunatic Asylum are on the website of the George Marshall Medical Museum: **www.medicalmuseum.org.uk**

MH 94 in TNA consists of registers retained by inspecting bodies from 1846 -1960. These include name of the patient, the hospital, asylum or licensed house, and the dates of admission and discharge, or death. There are also some patients' diaries in the series, which have more information on individuals' circumstances.

Chancery lunatics (see also the *Finding Records* sections in Chapters1 & 2). From 1853 the names in C211 can be searched by name. Before then, there is an index (IND 1/17612) covering 1648-1853. IND 1 contains indexes to a range of Chancery cases, the online catalogue will help to locate the one related to the series and the period needed.

The Clerk of the Custodies of Lunatics and Idiots kept a register of bonds given as security for the administration of a lunatic's income and possessions between 1817-1904 (earlier ones were destroyed). These are in J 103, filed in date order. In J 117 there are miscellaneous bonds and papers relating to all kinds of business, including some matters related to lunatics between 1707-1967.

Disputes or 'traverses' from Elizabeth I to Victoria are in C 206. There are remembrance rolls in C 221 and C 222, and writs in C 245.

C38 contains reports made to the court by the Chancery Masters about their investigations stored in over 3,000 boxes. There may also be supporting documents for individual cases. C 103-115 has other documents submitted to the court from, for example, petitioners. An index to these exhibits is available at TNA.

Decrees and orders relating to lunatics are in C 33, which contains 1262 volumes recording the decrees and orders made by the court of Chancery. They are arranged chronologically and run from 1544-1875. From 1876-1955 the entry books of decrees and orders in the Chancery Division are kept in J 15. Some decrees can also be found in C 78 and C 79. Both of these cover the period 1534-1903.

Court of Protection records giving authority to hold inquisitions, etc., can be found in J 80. There are also some records here going back to 1852 and they go up to 1956.

Bethlem Hospital casebooks, describing individual cases, start in 1816. The records are still with the hospital, which is now located in Beckenham, Kent and the records are still kept there. (see also *Finding Records* in Chapters 1 & 2)

Poor Law Union Records from 1834 should help to find out what happened to a poor mentally ill or disabled ancestor. These are in CROs or BROs. There is a series of Gibson Guides on the Poor Law Unions and what records they have. Annual returns had to be made from 1825-1889 of the mentally defective and mentally ill chargeable to the parish and passed to Quarter Sessions. There should be records both among the parish documents and in Quarter Sessions, so surviving records will be in CROs and BROs. The 1867 Metropolitan Poor Act required all the Boards of Guardians in London to have an infirmary, separate from the workhouse and the admission and discharge registers will indicate whether a patient was mentally ill.

Records of insane inmates in workhouses and county asylums were kept by the government between 1834-1909. Surviving records are in TNA in MH12 and are arranged by county and Poor Law Union. Some have been digitised and can be accessed through TNA's catalogue. There is also a sample of patients' files from county asylums between 1849-1960 in MH 85. These are closed for 75 years.

Census returns from 1841 will contain the inhabitants of asylums and private madhouses. How they were entered varies. A few, such as Cheshire County Asylum in 1871, gave full names. Usually, however, the inmates of an establishment will be listed by initials and occupation. At the County Lunatic Asylum at Fareham in

Hampshire the first name followed by initials was given. Some will also give birthplace. This may be enough, with information from other sources, for family historians to identify an individual. Confirmation should come from the admission register of an institution. For obvious reasons, the census enumerators did not wander around asking inmates their names, occupations and circumstances. Instead they simply copied the information from the establishment's records: patients are usually listed in the same order in the census returns as they are in the admission register. By 1911 names are given in full, except for those in Broadmoor. From 1851 the last column in the enumerator's return noted whether a person was 'deaf, dumb, blind or lunatic', which will help to identify those being cared for either at home or as single lunatics whose carers did not require a licence.

Paupers in Workhouses. This Parliamentary Paper, number 490, of 1861 was published. It is available in specialist libraries and also on CD-ROM (Anguline Research Archives, 2007).

Reports by the Metropolitan Commissioners in Lunacy were published as Parliamentary Papers. The first, the 1844 Report, is available through a number of websites. The others will be found in specialist libraries. They will give you an idea about the conditions in an establishment in which a family member was staying. Abuses in asylums are sometimes detailed in these reports. These might lead to court proceedings, which will be found in the standard criminal records and might also be reported in newspapers. Correspondence and papers of the commissioners and subsequent authorities from 1790-1971 are in TNA class MH 51. There are 846 separate files here, covering the whole country. MH 51/734 contains a list made in 1961 of institutions caring for the insane between c. 1201-1966. MH 51 737-762 has miscellaneous papers of the Commissioners in Lunacy between the 1840s-1860s containing lists of lunatics in asylums. Those who escaped from asylums are in MH 51/762.

Royal College of Physicians has in its library a list of the madhouse licensees in the London area with whom the College had dealings between 1774-1828.

Annual reports were published by many of the public asylums. These rarely include the names of inmates or staff, but if you know your ancestor was in a particular asylum, it is a good idea to check to see if there is a report which will give an idea of what life there was like. Copies for a local asylum may be held in CROs and BROs. The British Library, of course, has an extensive collection and a search of their catalogue will help to identify what reports were published. Specialist and university libraries may also have copies and some have been digitised and are on sites like Googlebooks.

Criminal records. Criminal proceedings might result from incidents of abuse or illegal incarceration in a madhouse or asylum. These will be found in the standard genealogical sources and perhaps reported in newspapers.

The Bank of England registers Abstracts are held at the Society of Genealogists cover the period from 1717-1845. They are indexed and digitised and can be accessed through findmypast or by SoG members on its website. The full text of the originals will be held in the court that proved the will.

GWR's Probate Books or Probate Registers are held at the Society of Genealogists. These 270 volumes show that while most transfers or changes came about after the death of a shareholder there are other reasons for change such as marriage, bankruptcy or assignment of the right to receive dividends or sell shares through Power of Attorney, often on behalf of Lunatics. The registers were compiled from 1835-1932 but some entries date back as early as 1806. The Great Western Railway Share Transfer Registers, also held at the Society of Genealogists, have been indexed and digitised with note of executors, administrators, lawyers etc as well as shareholders and beneficiaries and are available as SoG Data Online to members through the Society's website. Other companies which issued shares would face the same problems and it is a question of tracking down any surviving records. TNA has a research guide *Looking for records of a business*.

Wills and probate. The National Probate Calendar, listing testators from 1858-1966, is available on the Ancestry website but may also be held in district probate registries throughout the country. Copies of wills have to be applied for by post. There is no indication in these records whether there were any subsequent legal disputes. An account of how I discovered Amy Louise Hall's story and how I researched it appeared in the online magazine *Discover Your Ancestors* (January 2014).

Societies and Charities. A useful guide to finding organisations helping the mentally ill or disabled is the *Charities Digest*, published annually by Family Welfare Enterprises Ltd and available in the reference section of public libraries. It gives the date of foundation and the original name. If you need to find the archives, you can go to the website or contact them by telephone or letter. The Alleged Lunatics' Friend Society published reports from 1847 and the Lunacy Law Reform Association published its first report in 1874. Louisa Lowe also wrote *The Bastilles of England or the Lunacy Laws at Work* Vol 1 (1883), with examples of alleged abuses of the law.

GREAT WESTERN RAILWAY.

No.	PROPRIETORS.	Date of Demand	Probate, &c.	Date.	Name of Executors, &c.	Address.	Observations.

GWR report maintenance of fortune for lunatic and his family re Thomas Kirby of unsound mind to accountant general 1869.

Great Western Railway.

GWR stock transfer for Thomas Kirby of unsound mind 1869.

REGISTRATION OF PROBATES AND OTHER DOCUMENTS

GWR will abstract Peter Cator executor now of unsound mind 1914.

Great Western Railway.

No.	Residue	PROPRIETORS	Date of Probate	Probate, &c.	Date	Names of Executors, &c.	Address	Observations

GWR Will abstract Charles Kenedey lunatic replaced as executor 1864.

Further reading

Charlotte Mackenzie *A family asylum: a history of the private madhouse at Ticehurst in Sussex, 1792-1917*. Doctoral thesis, University of London 1986. Available online at: **http://discovery.ucl.ac.uk/13818277/1/388954.pdf**. Ticehurst was the most expensive and exclusive of the private madhouses in England so is in no way typical but this does give insights into insanity was perceived and dealt with.

Andrew T. Scull *Museums of Madness: the Social Organisation of Insanity in Nineteenth-Century England* (1979) looks at the growth of public asylums.

Sarah Wise *Inconvenient People: Lunacy, Liberty and the Mad-Doctors in Victorian England* (2012) details cases of abuse that lead to changes in the law.

CHAPTER FOUR
From World War I to the present day

Shellshock was what the troops in the battlegrounds of World War I called it. It was a completely new and unexpected condition: mental breakdown which manifested itself in a number of ways - paralysis, inability to speak or hear, blindness with no apparent physical injury or cause. Other symptoms, like nightmares, insomnia and depression, were more obviously mental in origin. It is likely that shellshock predates World War I, but was not recognised as a separate mental illness at the time. Other ancestors who became mentally ill after services in the armed forces might also have suffered from this. It is now called Post-Traumatic Stress Disorder (PTSD).

At first there wasn't much sympathy. Medical men called the condition 'war neurasthenia' or 'war neurosis' and it wasn't fully accepted as a genuine illness until about 1916. Sufferers were thought to be faking their symptoms to get out of fighting and some were court-martialled as deserters. However, it so quickly spread that medical men soon recognised that this was a genuine illness. By the end of the War, some 20 establishments had been taken over and over 80,000 cases had been treated. They ranged from full-blown mental asylums to convalescent homes, where those simply in need of tranquillity could recuperate.

The Maudsley Hospital was constructed at Denmark Hill in South London in 1915 to treat civilian mental illness but by the time it opened in January 1916, it was decided that it should be a specialist and research hospital for shellshock. In 1923, it went back to being a civilian hospital. In 1930, Bethlem Hospital relocated to Beckenham in Kent and in 1982 the hospitals became merged on the Beckenham site.

Royal Bethlem Hospital today.

Finding records may be a problem, not just because medical records are closed for 100 years but because the patient files from the major hospital through which most of the shellshocked passed have not survived. This was the Royal Victoria Hospital at Netley, near Southampton. There was a long-standing asylum in the grounds at the hospital in Netley, known as Block D. This was opened in 1870 by the British Army to treat mental illness among soldiers. Two rivers around the hospital led to the area being called Spike Island, and that was how the patients referred to it. In 1917 the authorities at the hospital called in Pathé to make a film about the condition and its treatment. Called *War Neuroses*, it is distressing to watch.

Almost all the English soldiers suffering from shellshock passed through this hospital to be assessed and then moved on to other mental facilities. Among the major hospitals pioneering treatment for shellshock were Moss Side Military Hospital at Maghull, near Liverpool, and the Maudesley in London, which had its origins in the neurology department of King's College Medical School. Craiglockhart Medical Hospital in Edinburgh was one of the few hospitals to use psychotherapy at the time. The war poet Siegfried Sassoon was treated here with daily sessions in which he discussed his experiences with a doctor.

Some of the treatments, however, were brutal and must have resulted in as much, or more, trauma as the original cause. Electric shocks were used on the part of the body affected. Another treatment was to force men to confront their fears: those who were afraid of noise where subjected to it. Other gentler treatments, like hypnosis and psychotherapy, were also used but these were less popular as they seemed to take too much time to work so men could not return quickly to the front line.

A Commission of Enquiry into Shellshock, chaired by Lord Scarborough, opened in 1920 in response to the ex-soldiers who were trying to claim disability pensions on the grounds of mental afflictions. The effects of PTSD may last for years, or may surface later in life, so it is worth considering whether a family member who became mentally disturbed when middle-aged or elderly might have been experiencing a delayed reaction to service in WWI.

Legislation and other landmarks

The passing of the 1913 Mental Deficiency Act (detailed in the previous chapter) had its most significant effects in the 1920s and 1930s, when the 'moral defective' definition was used to commit to asylums a number of people who simply transgressed social codes, like the mothers of illegitimate children, or lads who today would get a community order for shoplifting. This was in great part due to the Eugenics Movement, which started at the beginning of the 20th century. The aim was to improve the quality of humankind by encouraging the best people to have children. Along with this went a belief that if mentally defective people were allowed to breed the whole fabric of society would be undermined by those of substandard intellects. A surprising number of the great and the good of their age, like Winston Churchill and, surprisingly, William Beveridge, George Bernard Shaw, Beatrice and Sidney Webb and other luminaries of the socialist movement were to a greater or lesser degree advocates of this.

Sterilisation of the mentally ill or handicapped was rejected in Britain. Although today Germany is notorious for its policies, thirty-one American states, Canada and the Scandinavian countries all implemented this and the laws remained on most of these countries' statute books until the 1970s. In Britain, people in asylums and hospitals for the mentally disabled were segregated from the opposite sex and forbidden to marry. As these records are closed it will be some time before the full extent and nature of this attempt at social engineering is revealed.

In 1927 the East London Child Guidance Clinic was opened in Spitalfields. A year later another Child Guidance Clinic was opened in Islington, North London. In 1936 this latter was the first in the country to introduce child psychiatrists and educational psychologists.

The 1930 Mental Treatment Act introduced the concept of voluntary patients. Although people (like Mary Lamb in the early 19th century) had gone into madhouses when they felt the need, this Act introduced a formal method of admission into public mental hospitals and the development of psychiatric outpatients departments. The aim was to extend to the poor an option that had always been open to those who could afford to pay.

One of the most significant pieces of legislation in the 20th century related to insanity was the 1937 Divorce Reform Act. This allowed divorce on the grounds of a spouse becoming incurably insane. Previously divorce had only been possible if a person was proved to be insane at the time of the marriage. This law also permitted divorce on the grounds of habitual drunkenness, which was regarded as a form of insanity.

Following World War II, an increasing number of day hospitals were set up and local authorities opened day centres. In 1948 public asylums and many subscription and private hospitals were incorporated into the National Health Service (NHS). From the 1970s there was increasing emphasis on treating mental patients in the community rather than putting them into asylums. The huge Victorian asylums were gradually closed and many have been converted into luxury housing. The idea was to replace the old establishments with smaller units in general hospitals and 'care in the community'.

The 1983 Mental Health Act brought in what is called 'sectioning'. Instead of using detention orders, people who are considered dangerously mentally ill can be put into a hospital to be treated without their consent. The grounds for doing so are covered in different sections of the act, hence the term. The Act was amended in 1995 and 2007.

Treatments

In the 20th century the two divisions of treatment, the gentle and the shock, continued. Sigmund Freud (1856-1939) and his followers pioneered psychoanalysis, also called the 'talking cure'. This form of treatment encourages and guides patients to understand the reasons for their behaviour in the expectation that this will enable them to change. It works better with neurotics rather than psychotics.

More robust physical treatments include Electro-Convulsive Therapy (ECT), which was introduced in 1938. It can be seen as a development of the theory that giving the brain a good jolt would rearrange it and restore sanity. This treatment does have good effect on some people suffering severe depression but initially was used fairly indiscriminately. Other shock treatments to induce seizures in the brain, e.g. by drugs, were also tried. Insulin comas had a fashion. Numerous other forms of treatment have been developed over the 20th century and can be researched through books and websites.

Charities

A number of charities have been established to help ex-servicemen and women. Just after the end of World War I a charity, the Ex-Services Mental Welfare Society, was formed in 1919 with the aim of supporting and helping sufferers. In the 1980s, it changed the name it uses to promote its services to Combat Stress. The first Ex-Services' Welfare Society home, named Chartfield, was opened in Putney Hill in 1921. There are also numerous charities to help all sections of the population with mental health problems.

Finding Records

Information for this period could come from other family members but as mental illness is a sensitive subject for many of the older generations, this needs to be approached with care and tact.

Because of the 100 year closure rule on NHS records of individual patients, it is unlikely that family historians will be allowed access to the majority of 20th century records of their mentally ill family members. Most private clinics and treatment centres observe the same rule. Academic historians, however, may well be allowed to see them. Health records can be destroyed ten years after the last entry but some authorities have a policy of archiving them on film or recently by scanning. By a legislative quirk, however, workhouse records are closed for only 65 years and as workhouses existed up until 1 April 1930 when Boards of Guardians were finally abolished, family historians have to hope their mentally ill or disabled ancestors were accommodated there rather than in public asylums.

Courts Martial. Records of servicemen and women tried for breaches of military discipline between 1796-1963 are in TNA. Registers and other records for courts martial in Britain are in WO 92, which starts in 1666 and continues to 1960, with a gap from 1704-1806. There is also a register covering 1909-1963 in WO 213. Those conducted abroad between 1796-1960 are in WO 90. A list compiled by G. Oram and J. Putowski entitled *Death sentences passed by the military courts of the British Army 1914-1924* (F. Boutle Publishers, 2005) gives surnames and dates. Over 90% of sentences were commuted to other punishments. Other records relating to servicemen and women in World War I are available in the standard genealogical sources and there are various guides on how to use them.

Court of Protection. In TNA, J 2 has a 2% sample of papers from the Court of Protection from 1900-1983. J 79 contains files from the Supreme Court of Judicature relating to the sale of property and the disposal of investments of the mentally ill from

53

1904-1933. There are 615 boxes, arranged alphabetically, which must be ordered three days in advance.

Royal Victoria Hospital, Netley 1856-1990. There are some records in Hampshire County Archives, including administrative records, chapel records, maps and plans and photographs as well as miscellaneous printed material. Most of the collection is made up of photographs and personal material donated to the chapel museum by over 200 contributors. Netley Military Cemetery is part of the Commonwealth War Graves' Commission so the burials there are on the CWGC site: **www.cwgc.org**

Ex-Services' Mental Welfare Society retains it own records. **www.combatstress.com**

Divorce records from 1858-1958 are in TNA and have been indexed. There may also be accounts of the more interesting divorces in local or national newspapers.

Further Reading

Peter Barham, *Closing the Asylum: the Mental Patient and Modern Society* (1997) looks at the 20th century movement to move people from mental hospitals into the community.
Philip Hoare *Spike Island: The Memory of a Military Hospital* (Fourth Estate, 2001)
Fiona Reid, *Broken Men: Shellshock, Treatment and Recovery in Britain 1914-1930* (Continuum 2010). Academic study.

CHAPTER FIVE
Special interest asylums

From the 18th century asylums to cater for different occupations and sections of the population were created. The major ones were for employees of the East India Company and the armed forces.

East India Company

The East India Company had a charter to trade with India and Asia from 1600. Over the years many people went to its various centres to work and some, of course, became mentally ill. The first, privately-run, lunatic asylum for Europeans was opened in 1747 in Bengal. It was followed by one in Calcutta opened in 1787. This was run by the company but the services declined after 1818 and about this time a private madhouse was set up in Bhowanipur, Calcutta. In Madras an asylum was established in 1794.

The belief that environment influenced mental health meant that Europeans were seen as particularly susceptible to the tropical climate and from 1818 the Company began to send patients who did not improve within six months back to England. The money for their passage was advanced as a loan. Initially the Company placed its mentally ill employees and members of their family, who were also eligible for care, in Pembroke House in Hackney. The treatment here, as reported to the Commissioners in Lunacy in 1862, seems to have been the standard 'moral treatment' regime, keeping patients occupied with work and leisure activities, which included a daily walk, riding and skittles. Inmates were also supplied with a range of board games, newspapers and books. Some families, however, preferred to make their own arrangements and placed their lunatics in other private madhouses.

In 1858 the British government took over the East India Company. Asylums were proliferating in Britain at this time and the situation was mirrored in India. Mental hospitals were established in Patna, Dacca (today's Dhaka, the capital of Bangladesh), which moved to Tezpur in 1876, Dulanda (Calcutta), Berhampore, Cuttack, Colaba, Poona, Dharwar, Ahmedabad, Ratnagir and Hyderabad, Jabalpur, Berar (Elichpur), Benares, (Varanasi), Agra, Bereilly, Waltair and Tiruchirapalli. In 1871 there was an innovation at Madras (Chennai). This mental hospital was for both European and Indian patients - although they were placed in separate wards.

Back in England, the land where Pembroke House was situated was needed for railway expansion and in 1870 the Royal Indian Asylum was opened in Ealing. This closed in 1892 and the few remaining patients were transferred to the Royal Navy asylum at Yarmouth or to Coton Hill Institution in Stafford.

Naval lunatics

Haslar Hospital at Gosport, across the harbour from Portsmouth, was built in 1746 as a hospital for sick or injured sailors. It had a section for the mentally ill but from 1755-1818, the Admiralty used a private madhouse, Hoxton House, near Hackney in North London.

In 1806, the Admiralty created the Royal Naval Hospital in Yarmouth to treat the sick and wounded of the North Sea Fleet engaged in war with France. Later this became a barracks. It fell into disuse but in 1863 the Admiralty decided to extend the hospital there and use it as a naval lunatic asylum, to relieve pressure on Haslar, which was overcrowded.

Army Lunatics

Royal Victoria Hospital at Netley, near Southampton, was opened in 1863 for army personnel. An asylum in the grounds at the hospital, known as Block D, began to treat mental illness among soldiers in the British Army in 1870. Before this it is likely that individual regiments and families were left to make arrangements for their own people.

Migrant communities

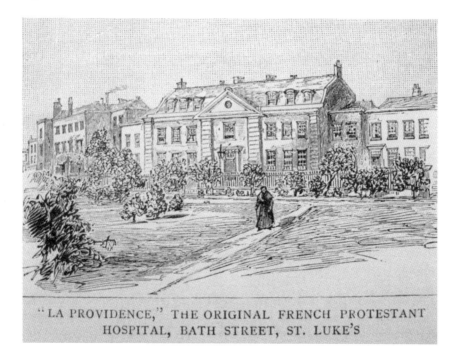

"LA PROVIDENCE," THE ORIGINAL FRENCH PROTESTANT
HOSPITAL, BATH STREET, ST. LUKE'S

La Providence.

Different immigrant groups also set up hospitals staffed by people who spoke their language. The French Hospital, known as La Providence, opened its first purpose-built establishment in Finsbury, London, in 1718. This was for those of Huguenot (Protestant refugees from France) descent. Until 1791 it cared for the mentally as well as the physically ill and infirm. The lunatics were housed in the 'Petites Maisons' or small houses. A few who were taken in had been discharged as incurable by Bethlem. Most seems to have been depressed, but some were a danger to themselves and others. After 1785, when the last was admitted, mentally ill Huguenots and their descendants in London went to the standard asylums: Bethlem, Guy's or St Luke's or into private establishments. For example, on 17 June 1875 the minutes record that:

'Charles Hurlin aged 79 and Joseph Cushway aged 69...were both considered to be in an unsound state of mind. It was resolved that steps should be taken to ascertain if such were the case, and if so to arrange for their removal to a Lunatic Asylum'.

Three weeks later on 7 August:

'With reference to the Surgeon's Report it was resolved that Joseph Cushway & Charles Hurlin...should be removed to Miles Lunatic Asylum Hoxton and that the Surgeon with the assistance of the Steward be desired to make all necessary arrangements'.

Another month passed, then on 4 September:

'The Surgeon's Report was read which stated that the two Inmates Cushway & Hurlin could not be received at Miles Lunatic Asylum on account of there being no room for them, it was resolved that the Surgeon should take immediate steps for their removal to one of the other neighbouring asylums'.

William Hurlin was 'Removed to Dr. Millar's Bethnal Green Asylum Cambridge Road on account of insanity and imbecility' on 9 September 1875. Later there are notes that Joseph Cushway died in Bethnall House on 25 November 1876. Hurlin died on 12 September 1877 but whether he was in the asylum at the time is not recorded.

Two other large migrant communities in London, the Germans and the Italians, had their own hospitals. The German Hospital in Dalston opened in 1846 and closed in 1987. The Italian Hospital in Bloomsbury was in service from 1884-1989. Both were intended for the physically ill, but it is possible that the records include some who also had mental health issues and were transferred elsewhere.

Friendly Societies

Friendly societies, groups of workers who banded together to create a common fund from which those in financial trouble and their families could be assisted, were established from the 18th century but were not officially sanctioned until the 1793 Friendly Societies Act. They kept sickness registers which recorded members or their families receiving assistance and also funeral money books, recording the name of the person to whom money for the funeral of a member or his wife was to be paid. The larger ones published journals and magazines. Most, however, excluded mental illness from the conditions covered and specified that relief was to be given temporarily, with a sliding scale over the first year of illness and thereafter a small flat rate for as long as the society's governing body considered necessary. There might also be a clause which denied benefits to those whose 'immoral or disorderly conduct' had caused their sickness. As some mental illnesses were thought to be caused by the individual's behaviour, this might be used to exclude a person and his family from long term relief, or even funeral expenses if the individual committed suicide.

Freemasons

In the 20th century the Freemasons maintained a general surgical hospital in West London. The Freemasons Hospital and Nursing Home opened in 1920 in Fulham Road. It moved to premises at Ravenscourt Park in Hammersmith in 1933 and was renamed the Royal Masonic Hospital. It remained there until its closure in 1996. The Freemasons did not have any asylums for their members, but at least one private madhouse was run by a Freemason. Dr William Perfect had an asylum in West Malling Kent from about 1758. It continued there after his death in 1809. Whether his patients were all Freemasons or not remains to be researched. Individual lodges may well have helped members and their families in need of mental health care and information will come from their records.

Charities

From medieval times almshouses were created by trade guilds, livery companies and charitable organisations for specific sections of the population, usually related to their occupations. Although mainly intended for the elderly and physically frail, undoubtedly some sheltered those who were no longer capable of administering their own affairs.

In 1885, the Soldiers' and Sailors' Families Association was founded to assist the families of servicemen. Since then other charities have been started. They are usually for particular sections of the Armed Forces, e.g. Royal Marines and will be found online.

Finding Records

Oriental and India Office Library in the British Library holds the archives of the East India Company (1600-1858), the Board of Control or Board of Commissioners for the Affairs of India (1784-1858), the India Office (1858-1947), the Burma Office (1937-1948), and a number of related British agencies overseas. The main records of the asylums are in IOR/K Records of Pembroke House and Ealing Lunatic Asylum, 1818-1892. These include medical certificates from 1830-1889; the Register of Admissions 1845-1892 and the Register of Discharge, Removals and Deaths 1845-1892. The casebooks from 1846-1892 are very informative. They include biographical details as well as descriptions of their mental conditions. Wills of employees of the company and their relatives are also held here. Disputes about wills may have been heard in local courts in India or in the British courts. A.J. Farrington, *The Records of the East India College, Haileybury, and other institutions* (London, 1976) gives further information.

Medical History of British India. Annual reports were published between 1867-1948 on mental hospitals in the various provinces of British India. There are copies in the Oriental and India Office Library. The National Library of Scotland's collection of medical records related to British India, which includes these annual reports, has been put on its Medical History of British India site. See: **digital.nls.uk/indiapapers/**. Any surviving records of the asylums themselves will remain in India, Pakistan or Bangladesh.

Census returns. The Navy used initials when listing 'lunatic' patients in earlier returns, but later became less squeamish about hiding the identity of patients in the Royal Hospital at Haslar. All are named in 1881 census. The Royal Victoria Hospital at Netley did not distinguish between the lunatics and the other patients, so all are listed with just their full names and army ranks. This makes it difficult to know why an individual was in the hospital.

Admiralty records are in TNA. The main ones containing information about mental patients are:

ADM 305 1755-1968 Royal Naval Hospital, Haslar: Miscellaneous Books and Records contains all sorts of documents, including some records from the lunatic asylum and also burial registers from 1826-1954. These are not just patients from the naval hospital, but include some military and even civilian burials.
ADM 102/415-420 has records from Hoxton House, 1755-1818.
ADM 102/356-373 has records relating to Haslar, 1818-1854.
ADM 105/28 has reports on naval lunatics at Yarmouth 1812-1832.
ADM 36 and ADM 37 hold the musters of ships, including sea-going hospital ships where naval personnel might be treated before they could be returned to Britain.

Haslar Lunatic Asylum. A return of all officers of the Royal Navy who have been admitted to the lunatic asylum at Haslar since its establishment in 1819 was made in 1842 and is in the House of Commons records. 1842 (586) XXVII.

Royal Victoria Hospital, Netley 1856-1990. Only some records have survived and are now in Hampshire County Archives, Sussex Street, Winchester, Hants SO23 8TH. **www.hants.gov.uk/archives**

There are no patients' records. What has been deposited include administrative records, chapel records, maps and plans and photographs as well as miscellaneous printed material. Most of the collection is made up of photographs and personal material donated to the chapel museum by over 200 contributors and the majority are related to World War I. Information about individual soldiers before WWI will come from the standard genealogical sources, like army records in TNA and regimental records in regimental museums, local record offices and the like.

The Commonwealth War Graves Commission site may help to local a family member who died in one of the armed services' mental hospitals.
www.cwgc.org

The French Hospital records have been published by the Huguenot Society in their Quarto Series, Vols LII and LIII, which are also on CD-ROM. This is an alphabetical listing of all patients admitted between 1718-1957, with details of their dates of entry and discharge, as well as extracts from administrative notes, e.g. about their behaviour. The original records are in the Huguenot Library and they are mainly in French up to the 19th century.
www.huguenotsociety.org.uk

The German Hospital records are deposited in two main archives. The archives of St Bartholomew's Hospital, West Smithfield, London EC1A 7BE. hold its administrative records. The Wellcome Library has miscellaneous records, including patients' notes 1890s-1950s. There are also a few articles and reports in Hackney Archives.
www.bartsandthelondon.nhs.uk/about-us/museums-and-archives/
  st-bartholomew-s-archives/
http://library.wellcome.ac.uk/
www.hackney.gov.uk/ca-archives

The Italian Hospital records are in LMA.

Friendly Society records that have survived may be in a number of locations. The larger societies, like the Ancient Order of Foresters or the Oddfellows, have their own archives. Information about others might be on the Registry of Friendly Societies' website: www.mutuals.fsa.gov.uk. TNA also holds records of some friendly societies from 1784-1999 in the series FS. The Friendly Societies Research Group, based at the Open University, may also be able to offer assistance, especially if you have information that will be of interest to them.
http:socsci.open.ac.uk/SocSci/socio/friendly.html

Freemasons. Records of Dr William Perfect's establishment, including his licence and patients' records, are in the Kent History and Library Centre, James Whatman Way, Maidstone, ME14 1LQ.
www.kent.gov.uk/kenthistorycentre

The general source of information about records relating to freemasonry is The Library and Museum of Freemasonry, The United Grand Lodge of England, Freemasons' Hall, 60 Great Queen Street, London W2B 5AZ.
www.freemasonry.london.museum

Almshouse records are in a variety of repositories. Many will be in CROs or BROs, other may still be with the administrative organisation or charity. Check the A2A website.

Charities details of these will be found in the *Charities Digest* and online.

SSAFA. Forces Help Central Office, 19 Queen Elizabeth Street, London, SE1 2LP.

CHAPTER SIX
The criminally insane

CHAPTER SIX
The criminally insane

It has always been recognised that some criminals are not sane, either permanently or at the time of committing an offence. From the Middle Ages there was a religiously based test - did the person concerned know the difference between good and evil? Depending on how dangerous these criminal individuals were considered, they were either allowed to remain in the community under the care of an approved person or locked up until a Royal pardon was granted. In 1542 it was decided that someone who was insane, or became insane before coming to trial, could not be tried, although it is not known what actually happened to individuals in this situation.

This 'good and evil' definition lasted until the early 18th century. In 1724 a judge created a precedent by telling the jury to acquit the defendant, who had shot at another man, because he was 'a man totally deprived of his understanding and memory, and doth not know what he is doing, no more than a brute, or a wild beast, such a one is never the object of punishment.' This changed the definition of criminal insanity from a moral one to one of defective intellect. The usual method of dealing with these lunatics was to make someone responsible for ensuring that they were unable to do any further harm. This often meant simply imprisoning them in ordinary gaols or sending them to Bethlem.

George III, who himself suffered from mental illness, was very sympathetic towards deluded souls who attacked him. Margaret Nicholson attempted to stab him in 1786 and in 1790 John Frith threw a stone at the monarch. Both were sent to Bethlem. This compassionate attitude extended to ordinary people. Mary Lamb was the second surviving child of a servant to a lawyer at the Inner Temple. Her father seems to have had a stroke, which prevented him working, and her mother developed arthritis. Mary had to take in sewing to help support her family and, as the only girl, was also expected to care for her parents and run the household. She seems to have suffered from bipolar disorder and in 1796 she stabbed and killed her mother. The inquest brought in a verdict of insanity and a surprisingly enlightened decision was made by the coroner, Thomas Phillips, to release Mary into her brother Charles's care after Charles assured him that she would be treated.

Charles placed her in Fisher House in Islington, a private madhouse. She remained there, receiving kind and affectionate treatment. Charles, a clerk, who himself had suffered mental problems, took on the responsibility of paying for her keep, one guinea (£1.05) per week, with some help from their elder brother John. After six months she was well enough to move to lodgings in Hackney and a year later she was able to rejoin Charles. They lived happily together, although Mary periodically returned to asylums when her mental health broke down. Brother and sister wrote (they were co-authors of the children's book *Tales from Shakespeare* and other works) and also entertained literary friends like Samuel Taylor Coleridge, William Hazlitt and William Wordsworth, until Charles's death in 1834. Mary lived to the age of eighty-two and died in 1847.

A few years later Mary's treatment would have been entirely different. Another attack on George III by James Hadfield, or Hatfield, in 1800 resulted in two Acts. Hadfield shot at the king at the Theatre Royal in Drury Lane. This action was precipitated by Bannister Truelock. The two men were religious fanatics and Truelock persuaded Hadfield that 'the Messiah would come out of his mouth' if the King died. The first piece of legislation passed by Parliament was the Act for the Safe Custody of Insane Persons Charged with Offences and the second was the Criminal Lunatics Act. Both gave the courts the power to confine people whose mental state made them potentially dangerous.

The first Act, specifically prompted by Hadfield's actions, meant that anyone who was acquitted of a serious offence because of insanity could be detained until 'His Majesty's pleasure be known', i.e. indefinitely. The second Act, resulting from Truelock's obvious insanity, allowed courts to detain people who were unfit to plead because of their mental state. Both men were sent to Bethlem. Hadfield was later transferred to Newgate after he and another patient escaped from the hospital. After eight years in the ordinary prison, Hadfield was returned to Bethlem as a criminal lunatic, where he spent the rest of his life.

These 1800 Acts resulted in more people being detained in prisons because of their mental condition. Often they were a danger to other inmates and the costs of the special requirements needed to ensure the safety of themselves and those around them were met by the prison. There were fears that parish authorities were encouraging the lunatics in their care to commit crimes so the costs of looking after them would no longer fall on the parish ratepayers. Eventually this led to the passing of the 1808 County Asylums Act, allowing counties to build their own mental hospitals. The Commission that recommended this legislation also said there should be a specialist facility for criminal lunatics but this did not happen for many years.

In 1808 Bethlem was in the process of relocating from Moorfields to St George's Field in Southwark. As part of the building programme, a dedicated wing for the most dangerous criminal lunatics was built. Men imprisoned there were encouraged to occupy themselves by painting, drawing, knitting, reading and playing musical instruments. They also carried out carpentry and decorating for the hospital. Bethlem remained the major asylum for criminal lunatics but space there soon ran out. Private asylums were also employed, mainly Fisherton House near Salisbury and the asylum at Camberwell in Surrey. They took criminal lunatics regarded as harmless.

In 1828 an Act 'to amend the laws for the erection and regulation of county lunatic asylums, and more effectually to provide for the care and maintenance of pauper and criminal lunatics' was introduced. This enabled justices at Quarter sessions to construct county lunatic asylums for people for whom private provision could not be made. The expense of building such an establishment would be met by the county's ratepayers and a committee of (unpaid) visitors would manage these asylums. As it was public money that would create such asylums on a voluntary basis, by and large the county authorities dragged their feet about implementing this. This meant that there was very little specialist provision for insane criminals.

Definitions of criminal insanity

In 1840 Lord Denman told a jury they must acquit the defendant if they considered that he was suffering from a disease of the mind and was 'quite unaware of the nature, character, and consequences of the act he was committing'. This was very similar to the definition created in 1843 and what is, with some modification, still used today.

Daniel McNaughten.

This development was produced by the case of Daniel McNaughton (or M'Naghten), who believed that the Prime Minister Sir Robert Peel was persecuting him and the government was trying to kill him. He came from Scotland to London to assassinate Peel but actually killed Peel's secretary by mistake. When McNaughten came to trial nine experts said that he was insane and the jury found him 'not guilty by reason of insanity'. Queen Victoria was unhappy with this verdict and asked the House of Lords to rule on this, because otherwise, she thought, people could kill anyone they liked and then claim to be insane. The House of Lords (which is the highest court in England and Wales) came up with a three-part resolution.

1. the defendant is presumed to be sane and that he/she is responsible for their criminal acts;
2. at the time of the crime the defendant must have been suffering 'under a defect of reason' or 'from disease of the mind';
3. the defendant must 'not know the nature and quality of the act he was doing, or if he did know it, that he did not know what he was doing was wrong'.

Queen Victoria also objected to the verdict in the McNaughten case that he was 'not guilty' and insisted that in future the verdict should be 'guilty, but insane'. After his acquittal McNaughten was transferred from Newgate Prison to Bethlem, where he spent 21 years.

Broadmoor

Despite the importance of the McNaughten case, it was not until 1864 that an establishment specifically for the criminally insane was built at Crowthorne in Berkshire and named Broadmoor. Since then both those deemed to be insane and dangerous when they commit a crime and those who become dangerously insane while in prison are transferred there. McNaughten was one of the first inmates.

Broadmoor.

Since the 20th century, there have been three other specialist criminal asylums, now called psychiatric secure units, created in England at Rampton at Retford in Nottinghamshire; at Moss Side and at Park Lane. Moss Side and Park Lane have been amalgamated into Ashworth at Merseyside. In general the records of these other institutions are not currently accessible to family historians. Most information about cases in the last 100 years will therefore come from newspaper reports.

Less dangerous insane criminals might still be sent to an ordinary prison rather than to Broadmoor. The Criminal Lunatics Act of 1884 required paupers who had served their sentences but were still mentally ill to be transferred to county asylums. The cost of care there was met by the parish where the offender was resident at the time of the offence.

Finding Records

Poor Law Union records should contain details of payments made to county asylums for the paupers deemed to be criminally insane. Any disputes about which Union had responsibility for support will be found in QS records and may supply more information about the individual. These will be in CROs and BROs.

Bethlem. Details of dangerous lunatics held in Bethlem Hospital can be found in TNA in the class HO 20.

Fisherton House Asylum records from 1813 onwards are in Wiltshire & Swindon History Centre, Cocklebury Road, Chippenham, Wiltshire SN5 3QV.

Camberwell House Asylum. Some records containing patients admitted between 1847-1888 are in the Wellcome Collection. There are also some clinical and patient records for 1846-1865 in the library of the Royal College of Psychiatrists.

Criminal trials. The City of London and Middlesex were outside the Assize circuits. Transcriptions of trials there from 1674 to 1913 have been put on line at: **www.oldbaileyonline.org**. Outside the Greater London area, accounts of trials will come from local and national newspapers.

Records in TNA. Most of the records relating to criminal lunatics held in TNA are in the HO (Home Office) series. Warrants authorising the transfer of insane criminals to Broadmoor or other asylums from 1882-1921 can be found in HO 145. From 1899 these volumes also have letters relating to criminal lunatics and staff at asylums.

Until 1876 there are quarterly returns of the patients in Broadmoor. These are in HO 8 which also includes quarterly returns of prisoners in convict hulks, convict prisons as well as criminal lunatic asylums. Details of names, ages and places of birth are included, as well as why they were in Broadmoor and how long they remained there. In 2008 the archives of Broadmoor itself became the responsibility of Berkshire RO. They are closed for 100 years. How to access them is explained on their website: **www.berkshirerecordoffice.org.uk**

There are some records in other series. From 1846, criminals admitted to an asylum or transferred from an ordinary prison are recorded in MH 94. They are arranged by year and then alphabetically. Records of insane prisoners in prisons and houses of correction were returned to the Commissioners in Lunacy for 1858 only, and are also in TNA in MH 51/90-207.

Further reading

David T. Hawkings *Criminal Ancestors* (Sutton Publishing, 2009) will help to trace any ancestor who was found guilty of an offence, including the criminally insane, and to track his or her movements between prisons.

Mark Stevens *Broadmoor Revealed: Victorian Crime and the Lunatic Asylum* (rev. edn, Pen & Sword, 2013).

CHAPTER SEVEN
Suicide while of unsound mind

Today it is estimated that between 87% - 98% of suicides are committed by people with some kind of mental illness or disorder. Depression and substance abuse, especially alcoholism, are the most common conditions linked to suicide. The inquests held by coroners to determine the circumstances and causes of death can provide considerable information about those of our forebears who killed themselves and how what they did was perceived.

Inquests

After the introduction of civil registration in England and Wales in 1837, there are two ways that show whether or not an inquest was held. The first, and more obvious, is when the death certificate states that one took place in the column which gives the cause of death. The second way is to look at who signed the certificate. If it is signed by a coroner, and his title will appear under his name, an inquest was held. Before this date, it is more difficult to discover whether an inquest took place. It is also difficult to discover whether an ancestor killed himself and what his or her state of mind was at the time.

Inquests were, and still are, held on those who have died in uncertain circumstances. The office of coroner dates back to at least 1194, when Richard II needed money to pursue his military career. The original job was to look into the circumstances around a death in order to ascertain whether any money or goods were due to the Crown, hence the alternative title 'Crowner'. Coroners were either elected for a county or appointed by a place with a privileged jurisdiction. Wales had coroners from 1282 when it came under English rule and Ireland after the 1800 Act of Union. Scotland has never had inquests (see Chapter 10).

Suicide was regarded as a sin against God, who gives life, and was a crime until 1961. A person who killed him or herself when sane was regarded as murderer, called a *felo de se*, literally felon of him or herself. Until 1871 the Crown or some other authorised body had the right to forfeit the goods and chattels, but not the land, of murderers and other felons, including suicides who were determined to be sane. If the suicide was found to be insane, he or she was not considered responsible for the death and so their property was not forfeited. Until recently, therefore, the jury's decision about the deceased's state of mind when they killed themselves had a great effect on many of the records relating to their burial and the disposal of any possessions they might have. An additional charge might come from the deodand. This was the object that caused the death, like a rope with which someone hanged himself. Originally it was supposed to be given to the Church in expiation of sin but the Crown soon started to appropriate either the object itself or its value. This medieval survival was not finally abolished until 1848.

In the past the jury took an active part in inquests, questioning witnesses and deciding who they wanted to call to give evidence. Until the mid-19th century it was considered a positive advantage if the jurymen knew the deceased and the witnesses so they could use their own judgement about them. As well as unequivocal verdicts, like 'temporary insanity', juries might also bring in an open verdict, like 'found drowned' or 'found dead'. This left the case open for further investigation. 'Found drowned' is often used in cases where the evidence suggests suicide because the jury wanted to avoid passing a verdict which meant the deceased would be denied a religious burial and their possessions forfeited. All well as being sorry for the deceased, jurymen were ratepayers and were well aware of the drain on parish resources that a family thrown into poverty would be.

They might also give a narrative verdict, which simply states what the jury believed happened, such as 'he died in consequence of having taken a quantity of laudanum but whether he took the same medicinally or with intent to destroy himself does not appear'. This had the same purpose: to ensure that the case remained open and, should more evidence later appear, further legal proceedings could take place. In such cases, it is worth looking for newspaper reports in following years. The person who took the laudanum, for example, may have committed suicide or been murdered and evidence might emerge sometime after the death.

The later 19th and the early 20th centuries saw a major reorganisation both of the coroner's role and jurisdictions. Privileged jurisdictions were gradually abolished and as populations grew new districts were created. Until the Coroners (Amendment) Act of 1926 there was always a jury but from that year coroners began to hear proceedings alone. There remain however, circumstances in which there must be a jury, such as when a person dies in prison or police custody. Before the 1926 Act, the coroner and jury had to view the body together but since then the jury has been able to decide whether or not they need to see it. However, someone - today usually a police officer - must still see the body with the coroner.

Inquest documents

An inquest produced a number of documents. The first was the inquisition, a sheet of paper, in later times often a pre-printed form, on which was recorded the deceased's name, the date and place of the inquest and the verdict. This had to be signed by all the jury. In addition, there would be notes of the witnesses' evidence. These are called the depositions and only sometimes survive before the mid-19th century. When the deceased was not known, and suicides often travelled some distance before killing themselves, the parish authorities might have handbills printed, describing the body and asking for help to identify the person. Some of these have also been preserved.

Until 1330, coroners had to give their records to the Eyre justices. The Eyre was a peripatetic court which travelled very slowly around the kingdom trying all sorts of matters. From 1330 until 1420 or thereabouts, papers had to be passed to the Court of Kings Bench. Between 1487-1752 coroners were supposed to pass their papers to the Assizes. The judges on circuit passed those that did not relate to murder or manslaughter to the Court of King's Bench (Crown Side).

With the arrival of Henry VII in 1483, following the expensive devastation of the Wars of the Roses, the country's resources needed to be replenished. Henry VII set up the Court of Star Chamber to find ways to maximise the Crown's income. Among other activities, this court reviewed inquest proceedings. To put it crudely, having a rich person who killed himself declared a *felo de se* was a nice little earner, so a verdict might be sent back to a jury with a demand for a different, more potentially lucrative, decision. Even deaths that were probably accidental were declared to be suicides and those who were plainly insane were found to be in full possession of their faculties. This means that if a family historian finds a well-to-do ancestor dying in unusual circumstances in Tudor times, chances are there will be a lot of documentation about it. As the Crown became more financially secure the court was less concerned with inquests and became more taken up with property disputes or official corruption. Between 1485-1642 inquest papers went from the Assizes to the Court of Star Chamber. The coroners in Middlesex (which had no Assizes) passed their papers directly to the Court of Star Chamber or the Court of King's Bench.

From the mid-18th century, most coroners became less conscientious about passing their papers to the Assizes. However there are some later inquest papers for the Western Assize circuit up until 1820. The Palatinates of Chester, Durham and Lancaster had their own Assizes until 1876.

Originally coroners were paid per inquest. From 1752 to 1829, they received £1, plus an extra 6s 6d in the case of a murder. They also got a travel allowance of 9d (nearly 4p) per mile to travel there, but nothing for the return journey. The fee was raised to 1 guinea per inquest (£1.05) in 1829 and from 1837 witnesses (including doctors) and jurors received payment for attending plus travel expenses. The coroner also received an extra 6s 6d for the work involved in paying out these amounts of money. Between 1752-1860 elected coroners had to pass their papers to the local Quarter Sessions, partly to reclaim their expenses and partly to ensure that any further action, like criminal proceedings if necessary, took place.

Burials of suicides

There is a further consideration for family historians. Parish registers record ceremonies, not events. They list burials, not deaths. If no burial service was held, the register might not include a person who was interred without a ceremony. Those found insane, or non compos mentis, could be given a Christian burial. However, until 1823 a *felo de se* suicide was not supposed to be buried in consecrated ground. Most were buried at a crossroads with a stake though their body. This pre-Christian ritual was intended to prevent the ghost of the dead haunting the living. The stake was supposed to anchor it to the ground but, should the evil spirit escape, at a crossroads it would not know which road to take and would remain trapped there. Some ministers, however, were willing to bury such suicides in the parish churchyard, but a service was not read over the body.

After 1823, *felo de se* suicides were buried in churchyards but there was still no service read over them. Some parish clerks noted these burials in the registers, others did not but everyone who was buried should be included in the day book, if it has survived. When researching all baptisms, marriages and burials in parish records it is worth checking whether there is a day book, which records the monies paid for ceremonies, bell-ringing, etc, and other information. Sometimes CROs list them with the registers, sometimes they appear with other miscellaneous parish documents. Churchwardens' accounts often contain similar information. Day books for burials may show how much the funeral cost, who paid for it, the name of the funeral director or undertaker, where the person was buried in the churchyard and often the cause of death. A cause that sounds like a verdict, either in the burial register or the day book, such as 'found dead', 'fell from his horse by accident' , means that an inquest was held. It was not for the parish clerk to record in a legal document that might be used many years later either his opinion or just gossip about how someone had died. Even 'lunacy' as a cause of death might suggest suicide

Attitudes towards suicides

Just as beliefs about insanity itself changed over the centuries, so did the beliefs about why people killed themselves. Deciding whether or not someone was sane when they committed suicide was not always a matter of medical evidence. There was often a strong social element in juries' verdicts, which family historians need to take into account.

There were also changes in the legal definition of insanity. For example, those who died in the commission of a crime, such as a burglar who fell from a roof, might have been declared a suicide. Those who died as the result of an accident whilst drunk might also be declared insane. Intoxication was classified as 'dementia affectata', i.e. acquired dementia. However, who was declared insane, which carried a social stigma, varied. For example in 1830 an organist in the City of London fell from his bedroom window whilst drunk. Evidence was given that, after being dismissed from his job, he had become depressed and taken to drink and the circumstances strongly suggested suicide. A few miles away in Westminster, a gin-drinking woman also fell from a window, apparently under the delusion the house was on fire. In neither case had anyone actually witnessed the fall. The first jury gave a narrative verdict, saying he 'came to his death by falling out of a window but what caused him to fall here is not sufficient evidence to show' while the second jury found that the woman had 'destroyed herself under a temporary fit of insanity'. Drunkenness in women has always carried a social stigma.

Felo de se verdicts seems to have been rare in medieval times, although suicide was strongly condemned as a mortal sin. Priests were encouraged to talk to the members of their flock who were in danger of falling into the sin of despair. As mentioned above, there were financial reasons for deciding whether or not a suicide was insane. The Crown had become richer by the time of Henry VIII (reigned 1509 -1547) so did not rely so much on the Court of Star Chamber. During his reign another element was added to the factors a jury took into account. This was religion. After the Reformation came Protestantism, which increasingly laid emphasis on the influence of the Devil. As late at the mid-19th century the verdict on a *felo de se* suicide said the person 'not having the fear of God before her Eyes but moved and seduced by the instigations of the devil' killed herself. The first full length book on the subject of suicide in English, *Life's Preservative Against Self-Killing*, by John Sym was published in 1637 and saw suicide almost entirely in religious terms.

By the 18th century, however, there was a widespread belief that to have committed suicide was in itself evidence of insanity. Religious writers fulminated against this but jurors went on returning verdicts of temporary insanity. *Felo de se* verdicts were generally reserved for people who had committed another crime, such as murder, or had transgressed society's codes by immorality. It was also quite usual for attempted suicides to be brought before a magistrate, because until 1961 suicide was classified as a crime. However, it is virtually unknown for there to be any further proceedings. What usually happened was that a member of the individual's family was asked to take responsibility for his or her care. Some of these people would, no doubt, have been placed in private madhouses. It was recognised that removing a person from the environment that had created their suicidal attempt would be beneficial. This more liberal attitude continued until the mid-19th century. There was a strong religious revival around this time, which again linked suicide to the Devil's work, so more *felo de se* verdicts seem to have been passed.

Coroner Wynne Baxter conducting an inquest into Annie Chapman, one of Jack the Ripper's victims.

Until the early 19th century coroners were almost always legally qualified. Thereafter medical men were increasingly appointed as coroners, like Thomas Wakely, founder of *The Lancet* and coroner for the Western Division of Middlesex from 1829-1862. He criticised lawyers, who had been much more willing to return open or narrative verdicts. Victorian doctors like Wakely seem to have been much more confident about commenting on the deceased's state of mind when summing up for the jury. Today coroners have to be both medically and legally qualified.

Suicide and insanity were both regarded as having an hereditary component so when someone killed him or herself, other family members would be regarded as potentially insane. This is confirmed by modern studies, which show that both schizophrenia and some types of depression are linked to genetic factors. Having a parent who committed suicide is also a strong risk factor. In addition to the potential taint of insanity attached to other family members, suicide was also classified as a crime until the 1961. This kind of social stigma did lead jurors to bring in verdicts which did not bring shame on a respectable family or on someone for whom they felt sorry.

Newspaper reports

Often the fullest accounts of an inquest are given in newspapers, especially from the late 19th century onwards and these are usually the best source of information from the 19th century until the middle of the twentieth. it is a good idea to make a list of the dates of death or burial of all ancestors and members of their families and check the local and county newspapers to see if there was an inquest which was reported.

County newspapers began in the mid-18th century. When they started, they had only a small amount of local news. Most of their coverage was about events in London, particularly proceedings in Parliament, but as time went on they started to cover local events. Most newspapers listed the inquests in their county, and published longer accounts of particularly interesting ones.

Local newspapers, which began around the middle of the 19th century, concentrated on a specific area within a county. They covered court proceedings of all kinds in detail so are in many cases the major source of information about inquests from the last quarter of the 19th century to the last quarter of the 20th century. The recent reductions in staff on local newspapers means that only the more dramatic inquests are covered today.

Whether the coroner is sitting with or without a jury, the proceedings have almost always been open to the public and therefore can be reported by the press. Broadly speaking, inquest proceedings concentrate on the circumstances and medical background and newspaper reports on what might be called the human interest angle. It is therefore worthwhile to investigate both. A really interesting death, like a dramatic suicide, might be covered in both the local and national press.

The coroner's records may not have survived and they will, in any case, usually only give the main points of the proceedings. Other evidence, though given in court, might not be included in the documents preserved by the coroner but may be reported in a newspaper. Where the witness depositions held with a coroner's papers can be compared to the newspaper reports, they seem to be the same so newspaper reports can be relied on for what was said in court. Where they need to be treated with caution is in what reporters were told outside the courtroom.

Finding records

The most important thing to establish when looking for the records of a suicide is to know in which jurisdiction he or she died. Jeremy Gibson and Colin Rogers' guide *Coroner's Records in England and Wales* is the best source of information to the whereabouts of surviving inquest papers. As mentioned earlier, each county will have one or more elected coroners but within counties there will also be privileged jurisdictions. These might be individual towns, Liberties or even individual Manors. This will affect where records may be found. Another Gibson guide will help researchers discover the names and dates of local newspapers.

Most surviving coroners' records after about 1750 are in the relevant CRO or BRO, but some have earlier papers. From 1752, accounts of coroners' expenses, which include names, verdicts and places, were submitted to the Quarter Sessions, and may be the only record of inquests taking place. These are usually found in the CRO. In some record offices they have been separated from the Quarter Sessions papers into an Inquests section, in others they remain with them. Coroners in a privileged jurisdiction, like the City of London or a borough like Dover, passed their papers to the recognised authority, which may have a separate repository.

Many surviving inquest records before the mid-18th century will be found mainly in TNA. See the research guide *Coroners' Inquests*. ASSI 66 contains inquest papers (1798-9 and then 1817-1891) from the circuits in Wales and Chester that went on handing in their documents after the other circuits ceased to do so. KB 14 contains inquests on prisoners who died in the Kings' Bench prison (1746-1839) and PCOM 2/165 contains a register of deaths and inquests at the Millbank Penitentiary between 1848-1863.

The Palatinate of Chester inquests are in CHES 18.

The Palatinate of Lancaster inquests are in PL 26 and PL 27.

Duchy of Lancaster inquests in the counties of Essex, Norfolk, Middlesex and Surrey, and in the Honors of Halton in Cheshire and Pontefract in Yorkshire from 1804-1896 are in DL 46. Inquests held in the parishes of Edmonton and Enfield from 1873-1888 are in LMA along with the papers from the Savoy from 1885-1888. Earlier papers from inquests in these parishes are also in DL 46.

Many medieval records have been published. If your medieval Latin is up-to-scratch, you can tackle the original documents in JUST 1, JUST 2 and JUST 3.

The Court of King's Bench was set up in 1200 and had two divisions. The Plea Side dealt with civil matters and the Crown Side with criminal matters. The research guide *King's Bench (Crown Side) cases 1675-1875* has information about inquest documents there. There are miscellaneous matters including inquisitions in KB 9 (Edward I-1675). In KB 11 there are indictment and other matter, including inquest papers from Assizes from 1676-c.1750 for counties outside London and Middlesex. Later ones from the Western circuit are in KB 13 (1748-1808).

The research guide *The Court of Star Chamber, 1485-1642* gives information about using the papers from this court. There is also a published handbook giving details on how to use its records up to the reign of Elizabeth I.

There are records of forfeitures of *felo de se* suicides' goods, which are scattered across a number of classes in TNA. Where they are depends on the period, the area of the country, and on other factors. In general, forfeited goods were the responsibility of the sheriff of a county. The series E 379 contains sheriffs' accounts of seizures up to 1660. Sheriffs' accounts and petitions, covering 1216-1837, are in the series E 199. The Special Commissions of Enquiries in the series C 205 might also be of use for the period up to 1870. Another class worth investigating is the Treasury Solicitor (TS). Set up in 1661, when the post was called Solicitor of the Exchequer, over the years many other duties were added and from 1876 these included the administration of some intestate estates, including suicides. There is a research guide *Funds in court* which explains the role of the Treasury Solicitor if someone dies without making a will. Relatives and even members of the community might sign a petition for the return of goods. Surviving petitions might also be with the records of, for example a manor, if the Lord of the Manor held the right to take the suicide's possessions.

Modern inquest records

Coroners retain control over the records in their jurisdiction for 75 years. After five years, they are usually deposited in the local CRO but are closed to the public for 75 years (or 30 years in the case of treasure trove). Relatives or family historians may be granted access to them on application to the coroner for the jurisdiction before this closed period is up. However, there are so many modern inquest papers that storing them is a major problem. Most can be destroyed after 15 years on the coroner's instructions. The exceptions are:

• all papers before 1875
• the indexed register of reported deaths
• papers related to treasure trove

- any which have a particular significance, for example an important legal, social or scientific factor
- murders

Unless the inquest was particularly important for one reason or another, the papers may well have been destroyed before the 75-year closure period is up and the papers are on open access. In these cases, information is most likely to come from newspaper reports.

Further Reading

Jeremy Gibson and Colin Rogers, *Coroners Inquests in England and Wales* (The Family History Partnership, 2009)

The website *London Lives 1690-1800* has a section on coroners' records, with illustrations of the types of documents that might be found. It also has some 5,000 inquests in London from the 1760s onwards.

www.londonlives.org/static/IC.jsp

Family and local historians are increasingly transcribing or indexing coroners' records in their areas. Try the Genfair site: **www.genfair.co.uk**

CHAPTER EIGHT

The mentally handicapped, the deaf and people with epilepsy

Mental handicap

Before the mid-19th century not much distinction was made between the mentally ill and the mentally handicapped until the Lunatics Act of 1845 brought in a three-fold definition of mental incapacity. 'Lunatics' were those who had periods of sanity. 'Persons of unsound mind' were those who from infancy were unable to manage their own affairs. 'Idiots' were those who were congenitally incapable to thinking or using their own judgement. Today the terms lunatic, idiot, mentally handicapped and mentally retarded are considered to have negative connotations and phrases like learning/intellectual disability are currently preferred.

The Lunatics Act further required that those who were dangerous should go into asylums and those deemed curable should be given treatment. Neither of these was a viable option for those who were mentally disabled. The National Asylum for Idiots stepped into this gap. It opened in 1848 in London and was the first facility in the country specifically for the mentally handicapped. From the 1840s, work on the Continent had begun to challenge the belief that nothing could be done with the apparently ineducable and the Asylum began to pioneer such work in Britain. John Langdon Down, a medical superintendent there, gave his name to Down's Syndrome, which he described in 1866.

As well as being the period of growth in asylums for the mentally ill, the 19th century saw the establishment of a range of institutions for the mentally and physically disabled, who were carefully segregated. The admittance process usually involved those who supported the charity by their subscriptions and donations nominating potential new entrants, who were then selected by ballot.

In 1848 a charitable establishment, the National Asylum for Idiots, opened in north London. It then moved to Colchester in Essex and finally, in 1863, to a purpose built establishment at Earlswood in Surrey. This was a charitable institution, originally intended for poor people. However, wealthier families started to request placements and private patients were admitted to subsidise the costs of treating the poor. Many patients did not remain here long; their families may just have needed what is now called respite care. Earlswood became a model for other institutions around the country. The Eastern Counties Asylum opened in Colchester, Essex, in 1859, followed by the Northern Counties Asylum at Lancaster and Western Counties Asylum at Exeter, both in 1864. Then came the Midlands Counties Asylum in Knowle, Staffordshire in 1868. These were all committed to making children productive members of society.

In 1889 a Royal Commission recommended that the blind, and the deaf and dumb, as well as 'the educable class of imbeciles' receive suitable education. Three years later the first school for 'feeble minded children' was opened in Leicester. The term 'feeble-minded' was used for the highest grade of mental disability. Imbeciles were defined as less capable and idiots were those most severely afflicted.

Caring for the mentally disabled

Probably the first establishment in the country to house the learning disabled, was the Magdelen Hospital in Bath. It was unique until the 19th century. Originally a medieval leper hospital, it had become a hospital for 'innocents' or 'idiots' by the 17th century. In 1854 the building was closed and it merged with the Bath Idiot and Imbecile Institution. This Institution in turn became the Magdalen Hospital School in 1887 and was later renamed Rock Hall School. It became part of the NHS and was closed in 1980.

Until 1834, at the discretion of the parish authorities, people could be given money to pay for the care of those who could not look after themselves because they were either mentally ill or mentally disabled. Many families would have been given help to care for their mentally disabled members. The 1834 Poor Law Amendment Act stopped this practice of 'outdoor relief'. Anyone who needed help had to go into the workhouse. This meant that many people who could have lived in the community with support were forced into the workhouse, where they became a substantial section of the long-term inmates. Some parishes continued to pay for private care but money could no longer be given to the disabled person's family. Some of the larger unions had contracts with private establishments or public asylums. Between 1885-1902 Fisherton House near Salisbury, which was used for 'harmless' criminal lunatics, also housed 'imbeciles' from the Westminster Poor Law Union.

The 19th century saw medical advances that led to the recognition of a number of syndromes with physical and mental symptoms. The most common of these is Down's syndrome. It was first described as a discrete condition in 1866, although it had been observed by previous physicians. It is likely that many of the children simply labelled 'imbecile' or 'idiot' had Down's syndrome. Heart and other defects are common, so many would have died young. There are many rare syndromes which were not defined until comparatively recently and researchers who can track down case histories may be able to discover the exact condition from which a family member suffered.

At the other end of the age scale, the elderly were expected to become forgetful. The terms 'senile dementia' or 'senile debility' or 'senile decay' are interchangeable and cover a range of conditions. Today we think of Alzheimer's Disease (first defined in 1906) but there are other causes. A stroke, for example, might cause damage to a person's mental function.

German measles, a mild and generally harmless disease, can have devastating effects if caught by women in the early stages of pregnancy. Babies may be born with damaged eyes, ears and hearts. In the worst cases, they are blind and deaf. Before vaccination was introduced in the 20th century, there must have been thousands of children born with what is now called congenital rubella syndrome.

Those who were more obviously physically afflicted, like the blind or those who could not walk easily (called 'cripples'), were not regarded as mentally defective. This does raise questions of how those with cerebral palsy were classified and treated. Cerebral palsy is usually the result of damage to the parts of the brain that control movement, although in a small number there may be a genetic factor. It might be caused during pregnancy, during a difficult childbirth or before the child is about three. The degree of damage can vary greatly. In some cases speech is affected and in about a third of cases epilepsy is also present. It is likely that some children with cerebral palsy were classified as 'cripples' while others with severe communication problems would be written off as 'idiots' or 'imbeciles'. People with cerebral palsy were called 'spastics', another term which is now regarded as unacceptable.

Following the Disabled Persons (Employment) Act of 1944, the Disabled Persons Employment Corporation Ltd, later Remploy, was set up in 1945 to provide employment for both mentally and physically disabled people, whether through illness or because of congenital problems. The organisation was owned by the Department for Work and Pensions and had factories making a wide range of products. It also helped to place people with disabilities in employment with other companies. In 2013 it was decided to close down the remaining factories.

Epileptics and deaf people

The novelist Jane Austen had an older brother who was cared for, along with an uncle, away from the family. Why these two were in need of care is not clear. They were possibly epileptic, but it may be that they were just deaf, since Jane mentions 'talking with her fingers'. Whatever the problem, the care they received seems to have been good. Jane's elder brother survived her by some 20 years, dying in 1838.

Using galvinism (electric currents) to treat epilepsy.

Although now not regarded as mentally afflicted, in the past both those with epilepsy and those who were 'deaf and dumb' were often regarded as insane and put into asylums along with the mentally disturbed. Epilepsy is the tendency to have recurrent seizures, usually called 'fits' in the past. These are caused by a sudden burst of excess electrical activity in the brain, causing a temporary disruption in the normal message passing between brain cells. There are many different types of seizure and the causes of epilepsy vary. Some cases are the result of physical causes or illnesses, like damage during a difficult birth, a blow to the head or an infection like meningitis, but the majority are still of unknown origin. Epileptic fits might also be called convulsions, especially in babies, but these were not always produced by epilepsy. In infants, they may be due to excessive heat or linked to teething. It was not until 1861 that it was recognised that epilepsy does not necessarily mean mental impairment. The first of the drugs to help prevent seizures was not discovered until 1912.

What is now the Epilepsy Society began in 1892 as the National Society for the Employment of Epileptics (NSEE). A 'colony' of people with epilepsy was created in Buckinghamshire where they would be able to work. Other colonies were created around the country. Men and women were kept strictly segregated and were not allowed to marry because it was believed their condition was hereditary. From 1909, children were admitted and they had their own special school. This school was closed in 1957 and pupils transferred to the National Centre for Young People with Epilepsy at Lingfield in Surrey. After World War I servicemen with epilepsy caused by brain injury also received rehabilitation here.

Because they were unable to hear and therefore copy speech, the deaf were regarded as 'dumb', i.e. unable to speak. They were assumed not to be able to understand. The first school for deaf children was opened in Edinburgh by Thomas Braidwood in 1764. It moved to Hackney in London in 1783. This was a commercial operation. The first charitable school for deaf children, the Bermondsey Asylum, opened in what was then a London suburb in 1792, but it also had places for paying pupils. Over the next century, 25 more institutions for deaf children were founded. In 1897 they became 'Royal Schools'.

Charities

British Deaf and Dumb Society (now the British Deaf Association) was founded in 1890. The Central Association for Mental Welfare (established in 1913) worked through local groups of volunteers to help mentally handicapped people. The National Council for Mental Hygiene (1922) had an emphasis on education and also stressed the social causes of mental illness. The Child Guidance Council (1927) set up the first child guidance clinics. These last three organisations merged in 1946 to become the National Association for Mental Health, which is now called Mind.

Most other charities for the learning disabled have been founded in the 20th century. The records relating to individuals will not usually be accessible. The National Association of Parents of Backward Children was formed in 1946 and in 1955 changed its name to The National Society for Mentally Handicapped Children' and opened its first project, the Orchard Dene short-stay residential home. It is now called Mencap.

The National Spastics Society (the original name of Scope) was founded in 1952 to campaign for the education of children with cerebral palsy. There was no charity to deal specifically with the deaf and blind until the Rubella Group (now Sense) was started in 1955.

Other charities set up to help children, like the Waifs & Strays Society, founded in 1881 and now called The Children's Society, and Dr Barnado's, founded 1867, had handicapped children among those they assisted.

Finding records

Parish and Poor Law Union records will be in CROs and BROs.

The records of Earlswood are in Surrey RO.
www.surreycc.gov.uk/recreation-heritage-and-culture/archives-and-history/ surrey-history-centre

The archives of the Magdelen Hospital and its successors are with St John's Hospital in Bath.
www.stjohnsbath.org.uk

Other institutions' records can be found through the Hospitals Database or A2A (Access to Archives) both on the TNA website.

Registers of patients maintained by the Union in imbecile asylums by the Westminster Poor Law Union are in LMA. Records from 1885-1895 are in WEBG/WM/52/1 and those from 1896-1902 are in WEBG/WM/52/2.

Remploy. TNA has various records relating to the Disabled Persons Employment Corporation Ltd and to Remploy Ltd 1945-2001. They are in the series BM and are mainly to do with the management of the companies but they include house journals in BM 6. Other records relating to individual factories and employers are held locally. Try A2A.

Down's Syndrome. Dr John Langdon Down's house, and later hospital, have been turned into Normansfield Theatre and Langdon Down Museum of Learning Disability, The Langdon Down Centre, Normansfield, 2A Langdon Park, Teddington, Middlesex TW11 9PS, which is owned and managed by the Down's Syndrome Association. There are some records here but the medical archives of Normansfield are held in LMA.
http://langdondowncentre.org.uk/index
www.downs-syndrome.org.uk

The British Deaf Association's archives from 1895-1963 are in LMA (LMA/4468 accession ref: B05/042). They include minutes, correspondence, reports relating to administrative matters, annual reports and accounts, journals and newsletters from 1878 - 2004. There is another archive of correspondence and papers in LMA relating to this Association filed with the papers of the Family Welfare Association (formerly the Charity Organisation Society in A/FWA/C/D/247/001. This collection is closed until 2024.

The Epilepsy Society's archives are held at LMA. Some documents relating to patients from Hampshire in the colony at Chalfont St Peter are in the Hampshire Record Office, Sussex Street, Winchester, SO23 8TH.
www.hants.gov.uk/archives.

The Queen Square Archive and Museum, UCL Institute of Neurology & the National Hospital, London WC1N 3BG holds archives belonging to the National Hospital for Neurology and Neurosurgery (NHNN) and those of UCL Institute of Neurology (IoN), including some papers relating to people connected with the National Society for the Employment of Epileptics.
www.queensquare.org.uk/archives

Mencap's headquarters retains its own archives but some local branches have deposited their records in CROs.
www.mencap.org.uk

The Children's Society's archives are being digitised. A selection is on
www.hiddenlives.org.uk

Dr Barnardo's Family History Service requires that the deceased person about whom information is requested should be a relative.
www.barnardos.org.uk

Further reading

Anne Borsay *Disability and Social Policy in Britain since 1750* (Palgrave Macmillan, 2005) gives a very useful overview of the development of specialist care and education for the mentally and physically handicapped.

CHAPTER NINE
Those treating and caring for the insane

A n ancestor or family members may have worked in an asylum or been involved in the care of the mentally ill or disabled. No qualifications were needed to nurse the sick, either the physically or mentally ill, until the 20th century.

Clergymen sometimes took into their homes individuals who were mentally afflicted. I assume that these were mainly people suffering from depression. A change of scene and the power of prayer would have been considered a satisfactory treatment. Alternatively, troubled and difficult adolescents might also be taken in. Family historians might find an apparently unrelated person staying for an extended period of time with a clergyman ancestor and it would be reasonable to investigate whether this was a patient rather than simply a visitor. Other carers were simply individuals or couples with a kindly nature who needed a source of income, like those who cared for Jane Austen's uncle and brother, or the woman who cared for Isabella Thackeray.

Professional bodies

What we today call a doctor was in the past generally called a physician. Physicians dealt with internal disorders and treated both physical and mental illness until the 19th century, when the specialisms began to diverge. Surgeons, who carried out operations, were originally barber-surgeons, proficiency with a razor being a necessary talent. The two occupations diverged in 1745, when the surgeons formed a separate Company of Surgeons, which from 1800 became the Royal College of Surgeons.

Under an Act of 1512, bishops could issue licences to physicians, surgeons and midwives practising in their dioceses. This system lasted until the middle of the 18th century: the last London licence, for example, being issued in 1767. Members of the Royal College of Physicians were exempt. This College was originally founded as the College of Physicians and received a royal charter in 1518. Its main functions were to license those qualified to practice and to punish unqualified practitioners or those committing malpractice. As well as physicians, the College regulated apothecaries, who mixed and dispensed medicines, what today is called a chemist or druggist. Apothecaries also had their own Society, founded in 1617, which operated until 1890. The Royal College of Physicians of Edinburgh received its royal charter in 1681 and the Royal College of Physicians of Ireland in 1654.

In earlier centuries medical practitioners were generally trained through apprenticeships and did not necessarily belong to the livery companies in London, Edinburgh or Dublin, unless they worked there. It was not until the 19th century with the growth of teaching hospitals that the majority of physicians took a more academic route. From 1858 they had to be registered by the General Medical Council, set up by the 1858 Medical Act to regulate doctors in the UK.

The differences between physicians and apothecaries were not so marked as those between doctors and chemists are today. Many physicians dispensed their own drugs and apothecaries might fulfill the function of a general practitioner today, diagnosing minor illnesses and giving remedies. There was no very great distinction between those treating physical and mental illnesses until the later 18th century.

Asylum staff

The Association of Medical Officers of Asylums and Hospitals for the Insane was founded in 1841 as a professional body for those responsible for medical care in both public and private asylums. In 1865 it became the Medico-Psychological Association (MPA) and received a Royal charter in 1926, becoming the Royal Medico-Psychological Association. It took its present title, the Royal College of Psychiatrists, in 1971. Branches in Scotland and Ireland were also formed.

The proprietors of madhouses were usually physicians, or at least were set up by physicians. These were often family businesses and later generations were not necessarily medically qualified. Most establishments were small.

In the more expensive private asylums there would be servants as well as staff used to dealing with the mentally ill. Of course there were abuses. Very poor quality, cheap meat and other foodstuffs might be provided to cut costs, or provisions might be sold or stolen by the staff, leaving the patients to go without but this was not typical.

In public asylums, the medical superintendents might only visit occasionally. They had their own separate practices as well and some ran private madhouses. The day-to-day work of the establishment was usually done by general staff, called in the 18th and early 19th century 'keepers'. This association with wild animals shows how the insane were regarded. After 1845 the term 'attendant' for men became the norm. Women were usually called nurses but men continued to be called attendants until the late 19th century, when 'nurse' was used for both sexes. Male nursing staff were preferred because of their greater physical strength. Both sexes worked long hours, often with the most difficult and sometimes dangerous people. Their wages were less than a farmworker earned. The perks were free accommodation, food and sometimes clothing. They did not have a good reputation. Inevitably some attendants abused their power over people whose mental condition made it unlikely they would be believed but it is only the bad that are generally written about, and often when some kind of reform is proposed. It is in the interests of reformers to paint as dark a picture as possible of what they want to change and campaigners emphasise abuses. Most people, then as now, seem to have been doing the best they could with limited resources. The minister of the Littlemore Asylum in Oxfordshire noted that the death of a female attendant (E.B) on 10 June 1862 'cast quite a gloom over the whole establishment'. She was 'kind, considerate, attentive and affectionate'. A tombstone was erected by subscription. Mary Lamb was well treated in the madhouse where she was sent after killing her mother.

Professional training

Although some private asylums, like The Retreat in York, had their own training schemes, those who worked in asylums generally had no formal training. They just picked it up as they went along. Those asylums that used the moral treatment model tried to employ those with a strong faith who could be spiritual guides, to bring patients to God.

Training for general nurses began in 1860 at St Thomas's Hospital following the principles of Florence Nightingale. A national training scheme for nurses was not introduced until the 1890s. The MPA introduced various qualifications for those working in mental hospitals and asylums. The first was the Certificate of Proficiency in Nursing the Insane, first awarded in 1892. After a three-month probationary period, candidates had to complete two years on-the-job training in an asylum. The syllabus covered basic physiology in the first year and then in the second year the management of physical and mental illness. Examination was by written paper and a practical.

The Nurses Registration Act (1919) established a register of general nurses. Supplementary registers for specialists, like mental nurses, were added. The first examination held by the General Nursing Council specifically for mental nurses was in 1922. Alternatively nurses could take the MPA's qualification. Those who held the Certificate for Nurses in Mental Subnormality, introduced in 1920, were also included in the supplementary registers. Anyone found to have behaved unprofessionally could be removed from the registers. It was not compulsory to be registered until 1943 and, as nurses were required to pay an annual fee to be on the registers, some may not appear before that year. The registers were published until 1968. In 1983 the GNC became the UK Central Council for Nursing, Midwifery and Health Visiting (UKCC) and was renamed the Nursing and Midwifery Council (NMC) in 2001. Under the Data Protection Act 2003, the Council is unable to give out personal information about those on the contemporary registers.

Many men, especially after World Wars I and II, came into nursing having received their training through military service. Initially the Army and Navy mainly employed surgeons because they were more useful than physicians on the battlefield. The RAF Temporary Nursing Service (now Princess Mary's Royal Air Force Nursing Service and permanent) was founded in 1918.

Trade associations and unions

An Asylum Workers' Association was formed in 1895 and in 1910 the more militant National Asylum Workers Union (NAWU) was founded. In 1931 it changed its name to the Mental Hospital and Institutional Workers Union and in 1946 merged with the Hospital and Welfare Services Union to form the Confederation of Health Service Employees (COHSE).

In 1943 the Society of Mental Nurses (SMN) was established within the RCN. It was limited to women nurses and was wound up in 1972.

Trade publications produced by associations and unions in which you may find mention of your family members include the journal of the MPA, which was established as the *Asylum Journal* in 1853 and then became the *Journal of Mental Science* from 1858. In 1963 it changed its name to the *British Journal of Psychiatry*. The early issues contain the names of those who passed their nursing examinations. The *National Asylum Workers Journal* was published by the NAWU but early copies are rare.

The Charity Commission

Between 1818 and 1837 a commission under Lord Brougham investigated the financial practices of charities in England and Wales. It is generally known as the Charity Commission but should not be confused with the statutory body set up under the Charitable Trusts Act 1853. The records of both the Brougham inquiry and the later Charity Commission will give information about charitable organisations, like hospitals catering for the mentally ill, where ancestors worked.

Bethlem was not included in the remit of the Metropolitan Lunacy Commission and indeed had managed to keep itself out of most of the laws regulating madhouses and lunatic asylums but it could not escape the Charity Commission and was investigated in 1815.

Finding Records

Of course the patients' records of asylums will include observations and notes made by physicians and staff members.

Proprietors of madhouses often advertised their establishments. Other information might come from bad publicity when some scandal erupted. These records will be found in local newspapers. Licences will be with QS records in CROs and BROs from 1774. TNA also has lists of asylums and their owners. See the *Mental Health* research guide and the Finding Records sections in Chapters 2 and 3.

Public asylum records will be found in a variety of sources. Consult the Hospital Records Database for their location.

Individual doctors' private papers and notes on patients may be in a number of specialist libraries, like the Wellcome Library or the library of the Royal Society of Medicine. They may also have been deposited with a professional association, like the Royal Society of Psychiatrists.

Censuses include the full names of staff, even if they gave only the initials of patients.

The Commissioners in Lunacy inspected private madhouses and public asylums. They published annual reports which include the names of staff in establishments. These are available online and in specialist libraries.

Asylum Workers' Association and *NAWU* records are both in the Modern Records Centre, University of Warwick Library.
www.warwick.ac.uk/services/library

Trade journals for the medical profession will be in the British Library Newspaper Library or specialist medical libraries. They may also be in the archives of the publication (if it is still available). The complete archive of the publications of the Royal College of Psychiatrists throughout its history are on the College's website.

Ecclesiastical licences will be found in CROs and DROs.

Bethlem records and staff salary books are in the Bethlem Hospital Archives.

Apprenticeship records will be found in the various livery company records in the City of London and in CROs and BROs outside the City. There was a tax on apprenticeship premiums between 1710-1808 (although there are a few records up to 1811) but this did not apply to those apprenticed to their fathers or another close relative or to parish and charity apprenticeships. The originals are in TNA in IR1. There are digitised images and an index on the Ancestry website and a digitised copy of the microfilm of the originals on both TNA and the SoG websites.

Charity Commission records relating to charitable trusts between 1817 and c.1940 are in TNA, class references CHAR 2 and CHAR 8. These contain of information on the activities and history of various organisations. They are indexed on geographical criteria and include the names of private individuals.

Oriental and India Office Library in the British Library holds the archives of the East India Company (1600-1858), the Board of Control or Board of Commissioners for the Affairs of India (1784-1858), the India Office (1858-1947), the Burma Office (1937-1948), and a number of related British agencies overseas. The main records are in IOR/K Records of Pembroke House and Ealing Lunatic Asylum, 1818-1892. These include medical certificates from 1830-1889; Medical Visitation Books (1860-1892) recording the visits of physicians; day books (1870-1892) giving staff salaries and various other ledgers and account books recording payments to staff and others doing work for the asylums.

Armed forces records are mainly in TNA, which holds records of the Army's medical services from 1800. As explained in Chapter 4, no records from the Royal Victoria Hospital at Netley have survived. There are research guides on line and books detailing the complicated army medical service records. Paybooks of Navy surgeons and nurses at Haslar Hospital 1769-1819 are in ADM 102/373-397) and Plymouth Hospital 1777-1819 are in ADM 102/683-700. The RAF's World War II medical services are in AIR 49 and operational record books for individual hospitals are in AIR 29.

The Army Medical Services Museum has information about the history of army nursing. The Royal Naval Museum and Archive and the Royal Air Force Museum also contain information about their medical services.

Further Reading

Peter Nolan *A History of Mental Health Nursing* (Chapman & Hall, London 1993).

CHAPTER TEN
Lunatics in Scotland

S cotland had, and still has, a different legal system from England and Wales. This chapter is necessarily only a brief outline of possible research avenues but family historians will need to understand the structure of courts and medical facilities in Scotland, as well as how poor relief was administered.

The earliest legislation, in the 14th century, divided lunatics into the 'furious', who were mentally ill and the 'fatuous', meaning the mentally disabled, later called 'idiots'. 'Furious' maniacs came under the custody of the monarch, who could 'coerce them with fetters', if necessary. Until 1897, the Crown devolved their protection to the Chancery, as in England and Wales.

The system of having a wealthy person declared incapable of administering their affairs in Scotland could take place in a number of courts. It could be the Sheriff Court, a burgh or Royal Burgh court, the Commissary Court (which dealt with ecclesiastical matters, including matrimonial cases and wills) or the Court of Session, which was the highest civil court in Scotland and so was also the civil court of appeal. From 1532, the Court of Session was the most likely court in which to find a case concerning mental capacity.

It was usually relatives who asked for a person to be declared incapable by reason of 'furiosity' or 'idiotry' by purchasing a brieve (= a writ) from Chancery, a legal document which required a judge to hold an inquest by jury to determine the case. It was the same process used to establish who was to administer the estate of a wealthy minor, so effectively Scottish lunatics were treated in the same way as children, as legal minors, whatever their age. If it was determined that a minor was mentally incapable, a tutor was appointed until a boy reached the age of 14 or a girl the age of 12. From then a curator took over to look after the individual's affairs. In the case of adults who were mentally ill, a curator was appointed. Both the mentally ill and the handicapped were usually entrusted to the care of a relative.

From the 18th century relatives began to petition the Court of Session rather than the Sheriff Court to ask for a 'curator bonis' to look after the welfare of someone who was incapable of looking after his or her affairs. In 1849 the Accountant of the Court of Session was made responsible for overseeing the administration of the estates of mentally incapable individuals, checking that those appointed to do so were carrying out their duties. In 1880 legislation allowed a Sheriff Court to appoint a curator bonis as long as the person's estate did not exceed £100 per annum.

The insane poor

The Scots did not adopt the full English Poor Laws and settlement system. From 1589 money to help the deserving poor and the insane poor was raised partly from landowners and partly through voluntary church collections. Church of Scotland parishes were legally obliged to support the poor and infirm who were either born in the parish or had been resident there for five years. From the 18th century, the free churches might also help members of their congregations. City magistrates were also empowered to impose rates on householders to maintain paupers and parish poorhouses were built in the larger towns and cities. The Poor Law Act of 1845 set up parochial boards, like the Unions south of the border, and these kept poor relief accounts. It became the responsibility of the Parochial Inspector to make provision for the dangerous or those without anyone to care for them.

Montrose Asylum.

94

Voluntary or charitable institutions played a large part in providing for the insane and the destitute. The first Bedlam in Scotland was built in Edinburgh around 1690. Other early charitable asylums were created in the larger towns and cities. The Montrose Lunatic Asylum, Infirmary & Dispensary was founded by Susan Carnegie in 1781 and the Murray Royal Hospital in Perth and the Crichton Institution in Dumfries were created by bequests in 1811 and 1839 respectively. Asylums were also established by subscriptions, as they were elsewhere in the British Isles.

Regulation and inspection of madhouses

Twenty-three Scottish private mad-houses have been identified in existence in 1855. Twenty-one were in the more densely populated central belt of Scotland. The 1815 Act to Regulate Madhouses in Scotland had very similar provisions to the English 1774 Act for Regulating Madhouses. In Scotland, however, it was sheriffs who had the major duty for supervising provision for the insane. They were responsible for the licensing and inspection of asylums in their districts, for making regulations for the asylums, issuing warrants to commit pauper lunatics and to investigate and free illegally detained lunatics. In 1828 the Madhouses Amendment (Scotland) Act made a warrant from the Sheriff for admission and discharge mandatory. There also had to be two visits a week by a medical practitioner if there were more than 100 patients in an establishment. The admission and discharge records had to be kept for inspection by ministers, JPs and sheriffs. A further Amendment Act in 1841 was mainly concerned with the custody of dangerous lunatics, but also required the keeping and transmission to the Sheriff of madhouse registers.

Proposals to introduce a similar Act to the English 1808 legislation which allowed the establishment of public asylums at the ratepayers' expense were fiercely resisted in Scotland. Following the revelations of ill-treatment made by an American reformer, Dorothea Dix, who toured Scotland in the early 1850s, the government was shamed into investigating provision for the insane. Between 1855-1857 the Scottish Lunacy Commission found evidence of substandard provision in private madhouses. In 1857 the Lunacy (Scotland) Act created the Scottish Lunacy Board, with two unpaid legal Commissioners for Lunacy, who themselves did not inspect institutions. This was done by medical men, who served as full members or assistants. The Act also made public asylums a statutory requirement and provision for pauper lunatics to be made from taxes.

Dorothea Dix.

95

The boarding out system

This feature of the Scottish mental health care system from the 1860s was unique in the United Kingdom. Instead of incarcerating people in asylums, lunatics were placed in private houses, financed by government grants. There were a number of motives for this: it was cheaper; it was a way of discharging people from asylums so others could be admitted; people could be discharged as 'cured', which looked good in official reports, and it was a way of providing what are now called 'halfway houses', allowing people to be eased back into the community. Whatever the reason, this system did have the benefit of preventing patients from becoming institutionalised. It was pioneered in Kennoway and the surrounding area in Fifeshire. Local people soon accepted this and it became a centre for boarded-out patients. There were, however, complaints when patients from Edinburgh were boarded out here. There was a proposal to use one of the northern isles, like Orkney, as a separate colony for lunatics but this was rejected. This system lasted until the early 20th century, finishing with the 1913 Mental Deficiency and Lunacy (Scotland) Act.

The criminally insane

Perth lunatic asylum was the first to be used for the criminally insane. It was originally built for French prisoners captured during the Napoleonic Wars. In 1842, the building began service as a civilian prison with a separate section known as the Criminal Lunatic Department. The local procurator fiscal was responsible for having the less dangerous criminals deemed to be insane committed to an asylum. It must be presumed that when an asylum was not available, the individual would simply be imprisoned.

An army hospital at Carstairs in Lanarkshire was opened in 1939. After World War II, as the State Institution for Mental Defectives, it treated the mentally disabled. In 1957 it became the State Mental Hospital and now provides treatment for criminally insane patients from both Scotland and Northern Ireland.

Mentally handicapped

The first facility for mentally handicapped children, Baldovan Hospital, was established January 1855 in Dundee 'for the Cure of Imbecile and Idiot Children'. Its name comes from Sir John and Lady Ogilvie of Baldovan, who were instrumental in setting it up. Queen Victoria was a patron, and donated £100. Later its remit was extended to mentally handicapped adults and today it is known as Strathmartine Hospital. The National Institute for Imbecile Children opened at Larbert near Falkirk in 1869.

Investigation of deaths

In Scotland, unlike England, Wales and Northern Ireland, there is no system of coroner's inquests, so accidental, unexpected, unexplained, sudden or suspicious deaths are investigated differently. The procurator fiscal makes a private investigation into the circumstances and then decides whether any further action is needed. This means that newspaper reports in Scotland are less informative than they are in England, Wales and Ireland where proceedings were, and still are, almost always open to the press and public.

In the case of suicides, forfeiture of moveable goods to the Crown (called 'single escheat') was the practice in Scotland. Forfeiture of land (called 'liferent escheat') was not used. Sheriffs were supposed to send annual reports to the Crown's treasurer, although this seems to have ceased by the early 16th century and there are only a few surviving examples before 1551. Thereafter, it was the direct responsibility of the Lord Treasurer to act when he was informed of an escheat. The forfeited goods were given to a person nominated by the Crown, often a family member, who paid a fee to the Exchequer for the administration of this 'donation'. Whether goods were forfeited or not depended on the degree and nature of madness exhibited by the suicide. Forfeitures peaked in the 1610s but continued until 1764.

In Scotland, Presbyterians had very simple burial practices: there was no formal ceremony or service, although a reading from the Bible and prayers to comfort the living might be said. There were no specific instructions about how to deal with suicides. Individual Kirk Sessions of the Church of Scotland might deny interment in their churchyards to suicides. There was no burial of suicides with a stake through the body. However, in the 16th and 17th centuries there are accounts of the bodies of suicides being treated like criminals by being hanged or thrown into water. Attitudes to and treatment of suicides did, of course, change over the centuries.

From the late 18th century, the best source of information about suicides whether or not the individuals were considered to be mentally ill will be local and national newspapers.

Wills and probate

Scotland's laws relating to inheritance divided property into two categories *heritable* and *moveable*. Heritable refers to freehold property or real estate and the laws about who would inherit were fixed until 1868. In practice an individual could only dictate what would happen to his or her moveable goods, i.e. cash and personal possessions. This means that it is far less common for wills to be challenged in Scotland, unless a testator's legacies were particularly valuable.

Finding records

From 1 April 2011, the General Register Office for Scotland merged with the National Archives of Scotland to become the National Records of Scotland (NRS), General Register House, 2 Princes Street, Edinburgh, EH1 3YY. Personal records in Scotland are generally closed for 75 years. In the past it was common for women to keep their maiden names after marriage, so it is worth checking for both names if researching a woman.
www.nrscotland.gov.uk

Court records, both Sheriff Courts and the Court of Session, are held in the NRS. There is an index to the appointments of tutors and curators for minors between 1701-1886. This includes the curators appointed to look after the interests of the mentally ill or disabled up to 1897. The index is arranged by the child or insane person's name. Before 1700, these cases are included in the Inquisitiones de Tutela.

The General Register of Lunatics in Asylums. 1858-1978 is in the NRS in series MC7. The register includes patients who were already in asylums when the register began so has those admitted prior to 1858. The earliest appears to be from 1805. The register includes: admission number, name of patient, whether a private or pauper patient, sex, date of admission, name of asylum, date of discharge or death, whether recovered or relieved etc., and a column for observations or comments. Each patient kept their original admission number, so it is possible to see if an individual went into an asylum or asylums more than once. Usually later admissions are noted on the same page. MC2 contains *Notices of Admission* which includes name, age, marital status, place of abode, nearest relative and notes on the patient's mental and physical health. The series HH (Home & Health Records) contains hospital registers. Access to records from the last 100 years is restricted.

The Scottish Commissioners for Lunacy published annual reports and their archives from 1857 are also in the NRS.

Records of individual asylums are usually held by the local Health Board. Consult the Scottish Archive Network (SCAN), which is an online catalogue of records in Scottish repositories.
www.scan.org.uk

Poor Relief records or parish and church minute books may include entries related to the mentally ill or disabled who were not put into asylums.

Criminally insane in Scotland are listed in the NRS, in HH 17, 18 and 21/48, and these records include casebooks and files from 1846. Series HO 8 in TNA includes quarterly reports from 1824-1876 of insane criminals in Perth Asylum. Records on criminal patients between 1931-1935 are held in the University of Dundee in THB 29, which contains the records of the Royal Murray Hospital.
www.dundee.ac.uk/archives

Deaths. Information about forfeitures from 1489 to the 19th century are in the Register of the Privy Seal. Between 1561-1649, they may also be found in the Register of Signatures, which includes applications by interested parties.

The report into a death and the findings of this report are passed to the Procurator Fiscal and noted in the 'Register of Corrected Entries' (or RCE) at the NRS. Records of deaths can also be found in the procedure books in AD9, which lists cases passed to the Crown Office and the outcome.

Wills, testaments and probate documents are in NRS. Digitised images of the testaments and an index are on: **www.scotlandspeople.gov.uk**

Local newspapers are held in the National Library of Scotland and local libraries in Scotland may also have copies. Many have been digitised and can be accessed on: **www.britishnewspaperarchive.co.uk**

Further Reading

Jonathan Andrew *'They're in the Trade…of Lunacy they 'cannot interfere'- they say':The Scottish Lunacy Commissioners and Lunacy Reform in Nineteenth-CenturyScotland* (Wellcome Trust, 1998).
Emily S. Donoho, *Appeasing the saint in the loch and the physician in the asylum:The historical geography of insanity in the Scottish Highlands and Islands, fromthe early modern to Victorian eras.* (PhD thesis, University of Glasgow, 2012). Can be downloaded as a pdf file from: **http://theses.gla.ac.uk/3315/**
Rab Houston & Uta Frith *Autism in History: the Case of Hugh Blair of Borgue* (Blackwell, 2000) follows a case in which a man's younger brother sought to have him declared an 'idiot'. This shows how such cases were pursed through the Scottish courts and incidentally has a lot of other information about family law and customs.

R.A. Houston *Madness and Society in Eighteenth-Century Scotland* (OUP, 2000) is an academic study of the law relating to lunatics; the definitions and treatments of and the attitudes to the insane in Scotland. It is full of details drawn from contemporary documents, including witness statements. There is a section in the book about the sources used, and the Bibliography includes various documents and their whereabouts. These make an excellent introduction to the law and the Scottish lunatic.

R.A. Houston *Punishing the Dead?: Suicide, Lordship and Community in Britain, 1500-1830* (OUP, 2010) is an academic study of how suicides were treated in Scotland and the North of England. It has an introductory section on the process of forfeiture which is a useful introduction to the records.

Tristram Clark (ed.) *Tracing Your Scottish Ancestors; the Official Guide* (Mercat Press 2011) gives more detail about sources of Scottish records.

CHAPTER ELEVEN
Lunatics in Ireland

The early turbulent history of Ireland left little time or resources for the establishment of a centralised system of care for the insane. Although England had nominal rule over Ireland from 1171 and some lords (at this time, of course, of Norman French origin) were settled there to bring Ireland under English rule, these men soon adopted the ways of the country and joined the local warlords and clans who controlled different regions. During this pre-Reformation period, the religious houses presumably provided care for the mentally and physically ill, as they did elsewhere in Europe.

In 1537 Henry VIII began the process of closing the monasteries and nunneries, which was completed under James I (1603-25). However, Protestantism never took hold in Ireland. The majority of the population have always been Roman Catholics ruled by a small number of Protestants, usually of English or Scottish origin and deliberately settled there to maintain Protestant control. From 1690-1829 the Penal Laws discriminated against Roman Catholics. The care system provided by monasteries and nunneries in other Catholic countries was absent and until the 19th century there was no system of poor laws to help the ill or destitute. Until the 18th century it is very difficult to know how the mentally ill or handicapped were looked after, or indeed if they got any care at all.

The first House of Industry, the equivalent of the English workhouse, opened in 1703 in Dublin following an Act of the Irish Parliament and five years later accommodation specifically for the insane was set aside there. The building of further Houses of Industry in the larger towns and cities of Ireland was achieved either by Acts of the Irish Parliament or through voluntary contributions. The Belfast Charitable Society, for example, was formed in 1752 and finally got enough to build a workhouse, which opened in 1774. In 1802 provision was made here for lunatics. As well as places for the unemployed, these Houses combined a number of facilities for the poor, the sick, the orphaned and the insane on the same site. In the 18th and 19th centuries the Grand Jury was the local body charged with the administration of a county and its responsibilities included the maintenance of local lunatic asylums and gaols. This was funded by rates levied on householders

As elsewhere in the British Isles, most provision for pauper lunatics was through voluntary and charitable sources. The writer Jonathan Swift, Dean of St Patrick's Cathedral in Dublin, for example, left money for the creation of a hospital for lunatics and St Patrick's Hospital opened in the city in 1757. For a long time, this was the only dedicated facility, although from the end of the 18th century there was a growth in private madhouses. Richmond Asylum, the first asylum specifically for the mentally ill, was opened in Dublin in 1815.

St Brendan's - on the site of the Richmond Lunatic Asylum which was opened in Dublin 1815.

In 1800, the Act of Union brought Ireland under rule from Westminster and the British set about importing their own systems. The Lunatic Asylums (Ireland) Act 1821 enabled the Lord Lieutenant of Ireland to create public asylums throughout Ireland. They were funded by a combination of central and local government. A public lunatic asylum in Armagh was begun in 1821. Nine more across the country followed between 1821-1833. This surprisingly made Ireland the first country in Europe with a public lunatic asylum system, even before they were made mandatory in England and Wales.

The English Poor Laws were introduced by an Act of 1838, which closely followed the legislation which created unions of parishes in England. As in England & Wales, workhouses were funded from local rates. In 1922 the Boards of Guardians were replaced by County Boards of Health or County Boards of Public Assistance.

As well as being the earliest state to create an asylum system, by the end of the 19th century, Ireland had become the country with one of the largest growth of admissions into asylums in the world per head of population. This was partly due to the way lunatics were admitted. The usual way was by direct application to the asylum, generally by a member of the lunatic's family. The other method was under the Dangerous Lunatics Act (DLA), passed in 1838. This applied specifically to Ireland. A person accused of behaving in an insane manner would be brought before two JPs, examined by a medical man and then, if found insane, committed to an asylum on the warrant of the Lord Lieutenant. The asylum staff could not refuse to admit individuals, even if they judged them to be sane. There was no requirement for proof and the allegation of insane and dangerous behaviour did not have to be substantiated by an independent witness. The underlying assumption was that all insane people were either dangerous or criminals and the scope for malicious accusations or to gain control of the property of a relative was extensive.

The Central Criminal Lunatic Asylum for Ireland opened in Dundrum, just outside Dublin, in 1850. It is now the Central Mental Hospital and continues to care for mentally afflicted criminals in Eire.

Ireland continued to be ruled from Westminster until 1923 when the Irish Free State was established, while the six counties of Ulster remained under British rule. From this point on, there are two systems in operation.

Finding Records

Unfortunately none of the genealogical handbooks on tracing Irish ancestry that I consulted had anything about medical records of any kind. This is therefore a very cursory account of possible sources of research. The major problem with tracing Irish ancestry is the destruction of the record office at Four Courts in Dublin in 1922. Some records, however, survived and there is also a system of local heritage centres in the different counties. If you know from where your Irish ancestors came, you can enquire at the heritage centres. Those in Eire maintain indexes and databases which are increasingly being put on the internet. Information from those that are not yet accessible on line can be extracted by staff for a fee. The Public Record Office of Northern Ireland (PRONI) was set up in 1923 and contains administrative records from that date and records from the six historical counties of Northern Ireland (Antrim, Armagh, Down, Fermanagh, Londonderry and Tyrone).

Lunatic asylums in Eire. These records from 1835-1900 are in the National Archives of Ireland and can be consulted by the general public. Ref. OPW/1/12 and OPW/2/12.

Lunatic asylums in Northern Ireland are included in the Hospital Records Database.

Chancery Lunatics. There are a few records relating to people in Ireland in the various Chancery records in TNA (See Chapters 1, 2 and 3). These relate to those who had property in mainland Britain as well as Ireland.

Censuses A very few records from parts of Ireland from the 1821, 1831, 1841 and 1851 censuses have survived and are in PRONI and/or NAI. Records of subsequent censuses up to until 1901 were destroyed by the government. The censuses for 1901 and 1911 are on line.

Poor Law records that have survived will be among local county records. In PRONI they are in the series BG. Those for Eire may be in a number of locations. Most are in the NAI or the National Library of Ireland (NLI) in Dublin but some remain in a local library or museum. See *A Directory of Irish Archives.*

Grand Jury records are not indexed and they contain a wide range of administrative matters, like the upkeep of roads, which were of more importance, on a day-to-day basis than lunatic asylums or gaols, so need to be searched carefully. They may, however, give information about people who worked in the asylums. There is an online leaflet, *Your Family Tree Series: 19* about them on the PRONI website. Surviving records are mainly in County archives.

The Central Criminal Lunatic Asylum records from 1850-1900 are 1900 are held at the Central Mental Hospital, Dundrum Rd, Dundrum, Dublin 14, Ireland. **www.centralmentalhospital.ie**. There are some administrative records before 1922 in TNA and after that date in the NAI. Police records relating to the crime for which a person was committed to the asylum are also in NAI.

Further reading and addresses

Mark Finnane *Insanity and the Insane in Post-Famine Ireland* (Rowman & Littlefield, 1981). Academic study.

Melinda D. Grimsley-Smith, *Politics, Professionalization, and Poverty: Lunatic Asylums for the Poor in Ireland, 1817-1920* (Notre Dame University, Indiana, USA, 2011). This academic dissertation is mainly about the administration of the asylum system and gives references to various other academic works on different aspects of mental health history in Ireland which may be of interest. It is on : **http://etd.nd.edu/ETD-db/theses/available/etd-12052011-142857/unrestricted/ GrimsleySmithM122011D.pdf**

S. Helferty & R. Refausse *A Directory of Irish Archives* (4th edn, 2003).

Public Record Office of Northern Ireland (PRONI)
2 Titanic Boulevard
Belfast
BT 3 9HQ
www.proni.gov.uk

The National Archives of Ireland (NAI)
Bishop Street
Dublin 8
www.nationalarchives.ie

National Library of Ireland
Kildare Street
Dublin 2
www.nli.ie

Jeremy Gibson, Brett Langston, Belinda W. Smith, *Local Newspapers 1750-1920 England and Wales, Channel Islands, Isle of Man* (The Family History Partnership, 2011).

Jeremy Gibson, Colin Rogers, Cliff Webb, Frederic A Youngs Jr, *Poor Law Union Records* (4 volumes): *Volume 1 - South-East England and East Anglia; Volume 2 - The Midlands and Northern England; Volume 3 - South-West England, The Marches and Wales and Volume 4 - Gazetteer of England and Wales* (The Family History Partnership, 2011).

Cliff Webb, *An Index of London Hospitals and their Records* (Society of Genealogists, 2002).

There are, of course, many thousands of books about insanity in the past and now. Histories of individual asylums and private madhouses can be accessed at a specialist library, like the Wellcome, or may be obtained through your local library. There are also websites where numerous out-of-print books, like 19th century annual reports of asylums, can be downloaded for free. Google books **books.google.com** and Project Gutenberg **www.gutenberg.org** are good places to start, but there are also many academic libraries, especially in America, that also provide this kind of resource. Put the name of the asylum , the county and a year of interest into a search engine.

The following will provide general useful background:

Catharine Arnold *Bedlam: London and Its Mad* (Simon & Schuster, 2008).

Paul Chambers *Bedlam: London's Hospital for the Mad* (Ian Allan Publishing, 2009).

Richard Hunter & Ida MacAlpine *Three Hundred Years of Psychiatry 1535-1860* (OUP, 1963) is now out of print, but a fascinating survey and anthology of theories about the causes of insanity and treatments.

Kathleen Jones *Lunacy, Law, and Conscience, 1744-1845* (Routledge & Paul, 1955).

William Llywelyn Parry-Jones *The Trade in Lunacy: a study of private madhouses in England in the eighteenth and nineteenth centuries* (Routledge & Kegan Paul, 1972).

The main commercial sites with digitised online resources for genealogists in England, Wales and Northern Ireland are:

www.ancestry.co.uk
www.findmypast.co.uk
www.thegenealogist

They all have some records, like the censuses, in common but it is difficult to keep up with what is being added and which records are held by one site but not the others. You can check without charges what resources there are and if there is something on a site to which you do not have a subscription, it is worth investigating if you can access it for free at your local library or another library, such as the Society of Genealogists.

The above sites will also include some Scottish records but the official website is:
www.scotlandspeople.gov.uk

Studymore
This is a Middlesex University resource provided by Andrew Roberts and is the primary site for all aspects of the history of mental illness, its treatment and asylums. Packed with information.
http://studymore.org.uk

Access to Archives (A2A) contains catalogues of county record offices and local archives.
www.nationalarchives.gov.uk/a2a/

AIM25 (archives in London and the M25 area) is a portal to the archive catalogues of various educational institutions, colleges, royal societies, businesses and local authorities in the London area, including various medical organisations.
www.aim25.ac.uk

Bethlem Royal Hospital Archives & Museum
Monks Orchard Road
Beckenham
Kent BR3 3BX
www.bethlemheritage.org.uk

British Library,
96 Euston Road,
London NW1 2DB
www.bl.uk

The British Library Newspaper Library's archive
www.britishnewspaperarchive.co.uk

Dango, the Database of Archives of Non-Governmental Organisations, resulted from a project to help researchers locate the archives of various organisations, including charities. Funding to maintain it ended in 2011 and, though the database is still operational, it is no longer updated or maintained.
www.dango.bham.ac.uk/Dango

The Hospital Records Database is a joint project of TNA and the Wellcome Trust. Information includes names of hospitals over their history; the year of foundations and closure (if applicable); types of records held on both patients and staff and their current whereabouts.
www.nationalarchives.gov.uk/aboutapps/hospitalrecords/

London Metropolitan Archives
40 Northampton Road
London EC1R 0HB
www.cityoflondon.gov.uk

Lost Hospitals of London
http://ezitis.myzen.co.uk/

Voluntary hospitals database (London School of Tropical Medicine)
www.hospitalsdatabase.lshtm.ac.uk/
Before the National Health Service began in 1948 many of the hospitals in England, Scotland, Ireland and Wales were within the voluntary sector. This database can be searched by name, county, borough or category. No specific mental hospitals are named. This website has statistical and other information about individual hospitals between 1890s and 1940s. It is mainly useful for background about where an ancestor might have worked or in the case of patients initially been treated. There is a link to the Hospitals Records Database.

Wellcome Library
183 Euston Road,
London NW1 2BE, UK
(part of the Wellcome Collection)
http://library.wellcome.ac.uk/

As well as holding registers of members, the following professional societies also have libraries which may contain records of establishments or private papers, etc.

Royal College of Physicians
11 St Andrews Place
Regent's Park
London NW1 4LE
www.rcplondon.ac.uk

Royal College of Physicians of Edinburgh,
9 Queen Street,
Edinburgh EH2 1JQ
www.rcpe.ac.uk/

Royal College of Physicians of Ireland
6 Kildare St,
Dublin 2,
Ireland
www.rcpi.ie

Royal College of Psychiatrists,
17 Belgrave Square
London SW1X 8PG
www.rcpsych.ac.uk

The RSM Library contains both books and documents, some dating back to the 15th century. It also holds the records of Society meetings. This is a membership-only library, but daily and half-day membership is available and there are free tours.

Royal Society of Medicine Library
1 Wimpole Street
London W1G 0AE
www.rsm.ac.uk/library

INDEX

About the SOCIETY OF GENEALOGISTS

Founded in 1911 the Society of Genealogists (SoG) is Britain's premier family history organisation. The Society maintains a splendid genealogical library and education centre in Clerkenwell.

The Society's collections are particularly valuable for research before the start of civil registration of births marriages and deaths in 1837 but there is plenty for the beginner too. Anyone starting their family history can use the online census indexes or look for entries in birth, death and marriage online indexes in the free open community access area.

The Library contains Britain's largest collection of parish register copies, indexes and transcripts and many nonconformist registers. Most cover the period from the 16th century to 1837. Along with registers, the library holds local histories, copies of churchyard gravestone inscriptions, poll books, trade directories, census indexes and a wealth of information about the parishes where our ancestors lived.

Unique indexes include Boyd's Marriage Index with more than 7 million names compiled from 4300 churches between 1538-1837 and the Bernau Index with references to 4.5 million names in Chancery and other court proceedings. Also available are indexes of wills and marriage licences, and of apprentices and masters (1710-1774). Over the years the Society has rescued and made available records discarded by government departments and institutions but of great interest to family historians. These include records from the Bank of England, Trinity House and information on teachers and civil servants.

Boyd's and other unique databases are published on line on **www.findmypast.com** and on the Society's own website **www.sog.org.uk**. There is free access to these and many other genealogical sites within the Library's Internet suite.

The Society is the ideal place to discover if a family history has already been researched with its huge collection of unique manuscript notes, extensive collections of past research and printed and unpublished family histories. If you expect to be carrying out family history research in the British Isles then membership is very worthwhile although non-members can use the library for a small search fee.

The Society of Genealogists is an educational charity. It holds study days, lectures, tutorials and evening classes and speakers from the Society regularly speak to groups around the country. The SoG runs workshops demonstrating computer programs of use to family historians. A diary of events and booking forms are available from the Society on 020 7553 3290 or on the website **www.sog.org.uk** .

Members enjoy free access to the Library, certain borrowing rights, free copies of the quarterly *Genealogists' Magazine* and various discounts of publications, courses, postal searches along with free access to data on the members' area of our website.

More details about the Society can be found on its extensive website at **www.sog.org.uk**

For a free Membership Pack contact the Society at:

14 Charterhouse Buildings,
Goswell Road,
London EC1M 7BA.
Telephone: 020 7553 3291
Fax: 020 7250 1800

The Society is always happy to help with enquiries and the following contacts may be of assistance.

Library & shop hours:

Monday	Closed
Tuesday	10am - 6pm
Wednesday	10am - 6pm
Thursday	10am - 8pm
Friday	Closed
Saturday	10am - 6pm
Sunday	Closed

Contacts:

Membership
Tel: 020 7553 3291
Email: membership@sog.org.uk

Lectures & courses
Tel: 020 7553 3290
Email: events@sog.org.uk

Family history advice line
Tel: 020 7490 8911
See website for availability